THE FACTS OF LIFE
and Other Dirty Jokes

The Facts
of Life

and **Other Dirty Jokes**

Random House New York

LIBRARY OF CONGRESS CATALOGING-IN-PUBLICATION DATA

Nelson, Willie
The facts of life : and other dirty jokes / Willie Nelson.
p.   cm.
ISBN 0-375-50731-0
1. Nelson, Willie, 1933–   2. Country musicians—United States—
Biography.   I. Title.

ML420.N4 A3 2002
782.421642'092—dc21
[B]   2001048480

Random House website address: www.atrandom.com

Printed in the United States of America on acid-free paper

2 4 6 8 9 7 5 3

FIRST EDITION

Book design by Barbara M. Bachman

I HAVE GIVEN A LITTLE THOUGHT to just what jokes would be proper or improper for this book. But, just a little. So, I would suggest that you read each one carefully, and then erase from your memory all the improper ones. Also, if you would just read every other word, they might be less offensive, and of course your reading time is then cut in half. However, for safety's sake, if you are a preteenager, please only read every third word. Thank you.

I CAN TELL BY THE
FEEL OF YOUR
THUMB THAT
YOU'RE A LITTLE
HESITANT TO TURN
THE PAGE . . .

THE FACTS OF LIFE
and Other Dirty Jokes

They say writing the first line of a book is the hardest part. Thank God that's over. Roger Miller said it must be true that the longer you live with your pet, the more you look alike. My neighbor came over this morning and chewed my ass out for shitting in his front yard. Thank you, Roger. I also have you to thank for the opening of my last book— "I didn't come here and I ain't leaving."

My daughter Lana just asked me if I wanted a couple of ibuprofen. I said no, I save my pain for the show. We are in Tulsa, Oklahoma, for a concert at Cain's Ballroom, where Bob Wills and countless other great bands have performed in the last fifty years. The last time we were here, we had to move it to a larger place because of ticket sales, so we decided to do two days at Cain's this time.

Lana, Kinky Friedman, and I are responsible for the contents of this endeavor, which is to be one-part song lyrics, one-part photographs, and ten-parts bullshit. That's where I come in. I seem to be doing very well. I have ripped off my friend Roger twice already, bragged about how well we draw in Tulsa, and exposed my daughter Lana for offering me drugs before the show. How do you like me so far?

"YOU DO KNOW WHY YOU'RE HERE?"

"Yes. There's great confusion on earth, and the Power that is has concluded the following: Perfect man has visited earth already, and his voice was heard. The voice of imperfect man must now be made manifest, and I have been selected as the most likely candidate."

"THE TIME IS APRIL, THEREFORE YOU, A TAURUS, MUST GO. TO BE BORN UNDER THE SAME SIGN TWICE ADDS STRENGTH. THIS STRENGTH, COMBINED WITH WISDOM AND LOVE, IS THE KEY."

✦

Where's the Show?/Let Me Be a Man

Explain to me again, Lord, why I'm here
I don't know
I don't know
The setting for the stage is still not clear
Where's the show?
Where's the show?
Let it begin, let it begin
I am born
Can you use me?

What would you have me do, Lord?
Shall I sing them a song?
    I could tell them about you, Lord
    I could sing of the loves I have known

I'll work in their cotton and corn fields
I promise I'll do all I can
    I'll laugh and I'll cry
    I'll live and I'll die
    Please, Lord, let me be a man

Please, Lord, let me be a man
And I'll give it all that I can
If I'm needed in this distant land
Please, Lord, let me hold to your hand

Dear Lord, let me be a man
And I'll give it all that I can
If I'm needed in this distant land
Please Lord, let me be a man

✳

LANA, DAVID ANDERSON, SISTER BOBBIE, L.G., and Gates are reg-
ulars along with me on the bus, Honeysuckle Rose III. Ben Dorcy is
not with us. Ben is now being preserved for trips in the near-Austin
area. At seventy-six-years young, he is cutting his world tours consid-
erably. But for all the millions of Ben Dorcy fans, Ben is alive and well.
Well, alive anyway. Thank you, Ben, for many years of faithful service

and wisdom—"*If you need a friend, buy a dog.*" We'll see you in Austin.

Cain's Ballroom was good tonight. The crowd was loud, which I like. The girls were pretty, which I like, and the guys were friendly. I forgot the words to "Crazy" and that's a first. Sammi Smith came by and sang "Help Me Make It Through the Night." Her son, Waylon, and Waylon's dad, Jody Payne, joined in on "Hey, Good Lookin' " and "Will the Circle Be Unbroken." Sammi's still singing like an angel.

On the Road Again

On the road again
I just can't wait to get on the road again
The life I love is making music with my friends
And I can't wait to get on the road again

On the road again
Going places that I've never been
Seeing things that I may never see again
I can't wait to get on the road again

On the road again
Like a band of gypsies
We go down the highway
We're the best of friends
Insisting that the world keep turning our way
*   And our way*

My dad, Ira; my mother, Myrle;
sister Bobbie; and me

Is on the road again
I just can't wait to get on the road again
The life I love is making music with my friends
And I can't wait to get on the road again

I wrote this song on an airplane with Sydney Pollack and Jerry Shatzberg. We were talking about needing a song for the movie *Honeysuckle Rose*. Sydney was the producer and Jerry was the director. So I said, "What do you want the song to say?"

Sydney says, "Something about being on the road."

"You mean something like, 'On the road again, on the road again, I just can't wait to be on the road again? The life I love is making music with my friends, I can't wait to be on the road again'? " I said the words kinda bland I guess, maybe without any feeling or emotion.

Sydney and Jerry kinda stared at each other, and Sydney said, "But what about a melody?" I said, "I'll come up with one before we get to the studio."

At the time, they were not that knocked out with the song. Of course, they couldn't hear the whole song like I could. They were very gentlemanly about the whole thing, not wanting to hurt my feelings and trying to act like they weren't worried.

THINK THE MORE I TALK ABOUT MY HOMETOWN, Abbott, Texas, the better. Not only is it the only hometown I have, it is by far the most educational spot on the planet. I honestly believe I learned more in my first six years in Abbott than I've learned since. Smoking, drinking, and cussing are definitely three subjects in which I excelled.

Miss Brissler, our next-door neighbor, and my grandmother, Mama Nelson (who raised me and sister Bobbie from the time I was six

I was raised by my grandparents
William Alfred and Nancy Elizabeth Nelson

months old), had already told us that if we drank beer, smoked cigarettes, and cussed, we were hell bound. At six years old I was well on
my way. However, the first songs I remember singing were gospel
songs. "Amazing Grace" was the first song I learned.

My first public appearance was in Brooken, Texas. We were at the
annual Brooken Homecoming, with all-day singing and dinner on the
ground. I was five years old. My poem was given to me by Mama Nelson to recite at the singing and performing part of "singing and dinner
on the ground." I guess I was nervous, because I started picking my
nose until it started bleeding all over my little white sailor suit, trimmed
in red. I did my poem . . .

What are you looking at me for?
I ain't got nothing to say.
If you don't like the looks of me
You can look the other way!

I have never had stage fright since.

There was always music in our home. My grandparents, Alfred
and Nancy Nelson, were both musicians. They took music courses
through the mail from the Chicago Music Institute. I could hear them
at night practicing their music lessons. My grandfather, Daddy Nelson,
was a voice teacher at one time, and they both knew a lot about music.
We lived in a little house on the edge of Abbott, and I could hear every
note they sang. I could also see the stars through the holes in the roof
of that house. It was all very beautiful!

Soon after that time, I was given my first guitar. Up until then I had
only written a few poems. Now I was able to learn to play guitar and
write songs. It was a Sears and Roebuck Stella guitar. The strings were

Mama Nelson and me in Abbott

very high off the neck, so my fingers bled a lot. But they eventually got tough. Kinda like life. . . .

My granddad used to sing:

> *Show me the way to go home*
> *I'm tired and I want to go to bed*
> *I had a little drink about an hour ago*
>   *And it went right to my head*
> *Wherever I may go, and wherever I may roam*
> *You'll always hear me singing this song*
>   *Show me the way to go home*

As you can see, I was getting a broad education.

Daddy Nelson was the kindest, wisest man I've ever known, unless it would be my dad, Ira. He never criticized a crazy thing I did. If my dad was ever mad at me, I never knew it. He would give me anything he had; money when he had it, advice anytime, plus he always kept my cars running like a clock. He was the best damn Ford mechanic that ever lived. Amen.

Me and sister Bobbie and some of the rest of the kids around Abbott, the Harwells and the Rajecks, we'd smoke anything that burned. We tried corn silks, cedar bark, coffee grounds, and grapevines before graduating to Bull Durham roll-your-own tobacco, and we did. That's where I learned to roll and why I can roll a joint faster than any living person. And then along came ready-rolls. No wonder I'm short. As much as I smoked, I should have been four feet tall. Thank God I quit cigarettes before I got lung cancer. Unfortunately, a lot of my friends and loved ones kept smoking. My mother, dad, stepmother, stepdad, and one father-in-law all died of lung cancer caused by tobacco. No

Sister Bobbie and me

one knew just how bad smoking was for you back then. If I had known, I would have quit at that time. But we thought it looked cool, smart, hip. Everybody did it. All the movie stars, sports stars (well, not all, but some), were always seen with a cigarette hanging out of their mouths. I love sports, and think I would have done a lot better if I hadn't been smoking cigarettes so early on in life, or not started at all.

As far as drinking is concerned, I had only tasted beer when I was six years old, but according to what I'd been taught, that was enough to send me straight to Hell unless I repented and asked forgiveness. So I did, every Sunday, for a long time. The preacher asked those of us who wanted forgiveness to walk down the aisle. I went down morning and night for years. I took no chances. Amen.

I believe we need all of the words we have. So cursing, or "cussing" as we used to call it in Abbott, was part of carrying on a conversation. Of course not in my home, but all over everywhere else. We told jokes, and we recited limericks.

> *There once was a man from Boston*
> *Who owned an American Austin*
> *He had room for his ass and a gallon of gas*
> *But his balls fell out and he lost them*

Abbott humor was somewhere between white trash and redneck. *All* words were important to us. We believed in laughter above everything. We laughed at ourselves, mostly.

We also loved to fight bumblebees in the summer months. The farmers down the road in Abbott would look for bumblebee nests while they were plowing and working in their fields. When they came into town, they would stop by Popps grocery store and leave word where we could find the nests. We would make our bumblebee paddles

Me, Ed Knapps, and the Rape brothers

out of apple boxes. They looked like Ping-Pong paddles with holes in them to let the air through and to swing smooth. Many Sundays I would come home with both eyes swollen shut from the beestings. Boy, what fun!

By the way, if you're ever stung by a bee, rub tobacco juice on it immediately. The pain goes away and it'll heal much sooner. However, you're still blind for a few days.

Another pastime in Abbott on Sundays, after bumblebee season, was placing an empty woman's purse on the highway that ran between Waco and Dallas. We would tie a string to the purse, then drop the purse on the road and run to hide behind a billboard. A car would come by, the driver would see the purse and slide to a stop. We'd pull the string, retrieving the purse before the driver in the car could get back to it. They were most always real pissed.

This made our Sundays special.

We still have a home in Abbott. We bought the house Dr. Simms used to live in. He's the doctor who delivered sister Bobbie and me. The house is about a quarter of a mile from where I was born. I go there when I can, and run and bike the same places again and again. They say you can't go back. Maybe they can't, but I can. Thank you, Abbott, for never changing.

Good Times

When I ran to the store with a penny
And when youth was abundant and plenty
Classify these as good times
Good times

When I rolled rubber tires in the driveway
Pulled a purse on a string across the highway
Classify these as good times
    Good times

Good times are coming, hum it, hmmmm
    Good times

Go to school, fight a war, working steady
Meet a girl, fall in love, before I'm ready
Classify these as good times
    Good times
Here I sit with a drink and a memory
But I'm not cold, I'm not wet, and I'm not hungry
So classify these as good times
    Good times

Did you hear the one about the duck that went into the bar, jumped up, and asked the bartender, "You got any grapes?"

The bartender said, "no," and the duck left. The next day, the duck returned and asked the bartender once again, "You got any grapes?"

The bartender said, "NO GRAPES."

The duck left. The next day, the duck came into the bar and asked the bartender, "You got any grapes?"

"NO. I don't have any grapes. I didn't have any grapes yesterday, I don't have any today, and I won't have any grapes tomorrow! If you ask me again I'll nail your damn feet to the bar!!"

The duck left. He came back into the bar again the next day, jumped up on the bar, and asked, "You got any nails?" The bartender said, "no." The duck said, "You got any grapes?"

Horsing around in Abbott

———

I LIKE JOKES. I like telling them, and I like hearing them. There are great joke tellers all around me. One of them is Poodie Locke, who once said, "You can't make a turd without grease," and "A farting horse never tires."

One of his latest hits around the crew bus is, "How do you change a dishwasher into a snowplow? Give the bitch a shovel."

It's hard to find good ones like that. Thank you, Poodie.

A HUSBAND AND WIFE HAD BEEN married for fifty years. Sitting around the breakfast table, the woman said, "Honey, do you remember fifty years ago today and we were sitting here after our wedding night? Sitting here at breakfast without any clothes on. Do you remember?" He said, "Yes I sure do." She said, "Do you think we could do that again? Sit here without our clothes on?" He said, "Uh, I guess so."

So they stripped off all their clothes. She said, "Honey I want you to know that my nipples are just as hot for you today as they were fifty years ago."

He said, "I don't doubt it, Honey. One's hanging in the oatmeal and the other one's in the coffee!"

THE SAME COUPLE had played golf every day for the past fifty years, and so on this day as they stood on the tee box, she said, "Honey. We've been married for fifty years today, so why don't we start off the next fifty years with a clean slate and confess all our past wrongs?"

He said, "OK. If you're sure that's what you really want. Do you remember seventeen years ago I had that blond secretary? Well, I had an affair with her."

The wife said, "Oh, that's nothing, honey. Before we met, I had a sex change."

He said, "Why, you lying whore! All this time you've been hitting from the red tees!"

KINKY AND LANA MADE A LIST of things for me to write about. Here they are:

1. RELATIONSHIPS—Yes, I've had some.
2. PAST LIVES—Yes, I just finished one.
3. KARMA—We deserve everything we get.
4. RELIGION—All roads lead to the same place.
5. POLITICS—Bullshit personified.
6. DAILY HEALTH REGIME—Keep breathing.
7. MUSIC BUSINESS—Very large.
8. FATHERHOOD—OK, but I think sometimes the mother should wear one, too.
9. THE ROAD—Which one?
10. SONGWRITING—No time. Too busy writing this fucking book.
11. GOLF—If you never have a bad lie, you never have to tell a bad lie.
12. MONEY—You will need some.
13. WILLPOWER—You will need some.
14. PERSONAL LOSS—You will have some.
15. MORALITY—A personal problem.
16. FAMILY—Absolutely necessary.
17. FORGIVENESS—Easy. Forgetting takes much longer.
18. PRIDE—One of the best country singers I know.
19. HAPPINESS—A state of mind.

My first girlfriend, Ramona Stafford

20. LONGEVITY—I come from a line of long-livers. My grand-mother's liver was . . . never mind, just keep breathing.

21. USA—Still the best place on the planet earth.

22. SUCCESS and FAILURE—Same number of letters.

23. MOTHER NATURE—Has a way!!

When we talk about the earth and the environment, we must remember the earth is a living entity. And just as our Bible tells us, "Physician, heal thyself," the earth is doing just that. It is healing itself. We shouldn't worry if the earth will survive or not. We should know the earth will take care of itself, and we will be the ones to strive for survival—by way of earthquakes, floods, hurricanes and tornadoes, washing away the poisons, the pesticides and chemicals that we put there. Our thoughts should be on our survival and praying we are not in the wrong place at the wrong time. Every action has an equal and opposite reaction. Whatever measure you hand out, that's how much you get back. The earth may be collecting old debts.

Other than that, we have nothing to worry about. But for some, it's already over.

✳ *Wednesday, March 14*

TONIGHT IS OUR SECOND NIGHT IN TULSA. It went very well with another wonderful crowd; a whole lot of young people, and a few my age and older. The bus ride to Victoria is long, about six hundred miles, I think. Rough miles. I used to think Texas had the best roads in the USA. No more. They're just as bad as everywhere else. I used to be able to tell when the bus crossed into Texas from Oklahoma, Arkansas,

Louisiana, or New Mexico, from any direction. I could tell by the feel of the road the minute we crossed into Texas, but no more, not now. All the roads are about worn out from the traffic.

Chet Baker is singing "My Buddy" from a cassette given to me by Jackie King. He knows how much I love Chet Baker. The other side of the cassette is Hank Garland, so I'm set till we get on down the road or I get sleepy. I think that might be soon.

Did you hear about the cook that caught his finger in the dishwasher? They both got fired.

It's getting late. . . .

Buddy

Laugh with me, buddy
Jest with me, buddy
Don't let her get the best of me, buddy
Don't ever let me start feeling lonely

If I ever needed you, buddy
You know how I really do, buddy
Don't ever let me start feeling lonely

I cry at the least little thing, buddy
And I'll die if you mention her name, buddy
Talk to me, buddy
Stay with me, buddy
Let's don't let her get the best of me, buddy
Don't ever let me start feeling lonely

Me and Zeke

Let's talk about things as they were, buddy
Before I got mixed up with her, buddy
Laugh with me, buddy
Jest with me, buddy
Let's don't let her get the best of me, buddy
Don't ever let me start feeling lonely

Zeke Varner was one of the best friends I ever had. From the time I was fourteen until he died last year, we were the best of buddies. We drank together and gambled together. Zeke played all games, from pool to poker to dominoes. He was an expert at them all.

The first time I remember meeting Zeke was at the Nite Owl in West, Texas. He was always one of my biggest fans. When I played with Bud Fletcher and the Texans at the Nite Owl, Chief's Bloody Bucket, Shadowland, the County Line, all the beer joints around Waco and West, Zeke was there every night.

For a long time Zeke and I worked for the Asplundh Tree Company, a company that trimmed the trees from around the high line wires for Texas Power and Light Company. My job was usually running the chipper, a machine designed to grind up all the brush from the trees we'd trimmed. One day, the boys up in a tree wanted a rope, so I climbed the tree and took them a rope. This was to be used by the tree trimmers to climb down after they were through, and to hand down any limbs that might be too large to just drop from the tree tops.

We were about forty feet off the ground, up above the high line wires. I decided to climb down the rope to the ground, which was usually a piece of cake. Ha! About four feet down the rope, and just out of reach from any possible help, I became tangled up in the rope. The rope was caught around one hand and I was stuck. I couldn't go up or down.

Bud Fletcher and the Texans, (left to right)
Willie, Bobbie, Linda Turner, Jody Andrews,
Laurence Dukas, Gerald Perkins, Bud Fletcher,
and Ira Nelson

After a lot of arguing, I talked Billy Bressier, my good buddy, just above me, into cutting the rope with his pocket knife. He didn't want to do it because we were forty feet up in the air, above some very hot high line wires. He knew that I could fall on them and die like the fucking idiot I was. However, since my fingers were leaving my hand, and the pain was unbearable, I decided on gambling that I'd fall between two high line wires.

Billy cut the rope. I fell exactly between two high lines, hit the ground, got up, and walked away from that job and never went back.

ZEKE AND I HAD BEEN out drinking, and stopped at Scotty's Club, one of the nicer beer joints on the highway. In West, Texas, the band played there every weekend. Guy Scott, the club's owner, was also a great friend and employer.

Scotty was watching a prize fighter on TV, the *Friday Night Fights*, I think. This night there was a guy at the bar that I recognized as a local gambler. Dominoes were his specialty, but he would bet on anything. So would I. The fight was in the fifth round, with five to go. "I'll bet thirty dollars on the guy in the black trunks," the hustler at the bar said.

I said, "You're covered!"

The only problem was I didn't have thirty dollars. I didn't have one dollar in my pocket. I could see Zeke's face flush a little. He knew I was broke. My guy won the fight and the hustler paid off like a slot machine.

On the way home, Zeke asked me what I would have done if the fighter in the black trunks had lost. "I'd have thought of something," I heard myself say. But I never gave losing a thought. I felt lucky and I was. I still am. They say, "Give a man a little luck and shit will do for brains."

*Me; my first wife, Martha; and some of the band
at Scotty's*

I have had more dumb luck than anybody I know. There must be a covey of guardian angels working twenty-four hours a day looking after me. I know I've given them a few anxious moments.

Like the night when I first got to Nashville that I laid down in the middle of Broadway, waiting to get run over. It didn't happen. Not a lot of traffic at 4:00 A.M. I could swear they were keeping me alive just to see what I'd get into next. I'm glad they feel that way. I'm trying to help them a little more these days.

No Place for Me

Your love is as cold
As the north wind that blows
And the river that runs to the sea
How can I go on
When my only love is gone
I can see this is no place for me

The light in your eyes is still shining
It shines but it don't shine for me
It's a story so old
Another love grown cold
I can see this is no place for me

Zeke had a place in Hillsboro, Texas, just ten miles north of Abbott. We all played poker there—Carl Cornelus, Steve Gilcrest, Johnny Holman, Albert, and Caroline, a gal from Malone who ran a poker game of

her own but loved to play at Zeke's Westside Social Club. It was after one of these all-night poker games at Zeke's that I got busted.

I had pulled over in Hewitt, just south of Waco, to sleep an hour or two. There was a lot of fog that night and it really wasn't too safe to drive. The next thing I know I'm on my way to the Waco jail.

Two local deputies had seen my car parked and decided to check me out. They said they saw me asleep in the backseat, and then saw something that looked like a joint in the ashtray. Later in court, it was proven they had no probable cause to search the car. One of the arresting officers didn't even show up at the hearing. He had already been fired for other reasons. Then my good friend Sheriff Jack Harwell spoke up for me. I could not have had a better character witness.

The jury decided there wasn't enough reason for a search, and dropped all the charges. I felt like I was well treated in Waco.

Zeke, Steve, Carl, Albert, Johnny, and Caroline all showed up for every minute of the ordeal. They were, and still are, my friends.

Once, Zeke was working as the night manager of a twenty-four-hour truck stop on Interstate 35, just south of Waco. He had a bad back and needed an operation but didn't have the money. But he had a plan.

He would pretend to fall off the stool at the coffee bar and collect enough insurance to get his back fixed. There were a few people down at the other end of the counter, and Zeke's plan was to wait until one of them was watching and then fall off the stool and pretend to have hurt his back, all with an eyewitness to the whole thing.

Just as Zeke saw someone start to turn his way, he fell off the stool. Unfortunately, no one saw him fall, so he had to fall off again. They saw him the second time and he successfully sued the insurance company and collected the money. He never did get his back fixed.

Sister Bobbie Lee
and me, 1946

Years later, he went to the doctor for some pain pills. The doctor said he had some pills that were pretty good, but these red ones over here, they are the best. But they can be addictive. Zeke said, "Doc. I am seventy years old. I'm addicted to nicotine, alcohol, caffeine, and a dozen other things. What's one more?"

We were really good domino players, especially as a team. We would challenge anybody anywhere to a game. We seldom lost. Except that time we were invited to play in the Luckenbach World Champion Domino Tournament.

They had heard Zeke and I thought we were very good. We went over there with a pocket full of money—wanting to bet it all—knowing we would win. We played two gentlemen about seventy-five or eighty years young. I asked one of them how long he'd been playing dominoes. He said, "I ain't never stopped."

I asked how much he wanted to play for, thinking at least a hundred dollars a game. One of the old guys said, "We play for fifty cents a game, and pay off after every game."

They each had their wives with them. One sat in between me and the gentleman on my right, her husband. She could see my hand, and his. I'm not saying she did anything wrong, but it seemed to me that every time he would pick up a domino, she would nudge him, ever so slightly, under the table with her knee.

It was a three-game series, and they won three in a row and a dollar and a half. We had been beaten by the best. I had to admire the way they all worked together. Other married people could learn a lot from those sweet folks, especially how to beat the pants off two younger, would-be hustlers.

Oh well. You win some and you lose some, and some get rained out.

On the way back to Austin from Luckenbach, we got pulled over by the highway patrol. When I got out, smoke just kind of rolled out with me. Lots of smoke. The officer was writing me out a ticket for speeding. After he stopped coughing, he said, "Willie, when are you gonna grow up?"

I guess I never will. I hope I never do. Amen.

✷ *Next day . . . Victoria, Texas*

So FAR, VICTORIA IS NICE AND UNEVENTFUL. My kind of day. The TV show is about chain gangs and how they used to sell their urine to leather-tanning companies. I've heard that some of the leather from Mexico, saddles and belts, etc., have been treated with burro piss. Kinda makes you think. I could have picked up a little more money when I was a young saddle maker at Ozark Leather Company in Waco. Oh well. Maybe it's not too late. The age of the urinator may even make it stronger and serve as a better and longer-lasting protection for the leather. I guess storage could be a problem on the bus. Maybe all the band buses could empty everything into one huge tank somewhere, maybe around Abbott. Or even better, we could go to all the farmers and ranchers and pee directly on their cattle. Now if all the bands all over the country were to do this, the farmers and ranchers could sell their cattle as already-seasoned leather. The extra income would be staggering.

On anger and abuse of a friend . . .

ONCE YOU HAVE YELLED and screamed at your friend on an unimportant matter or even an important matter, you must admit that you are a fucking idiot and apologize immediately. Sorry, Mark!!

Joe Massey and the Frontiersmen
(I'm fourth from left)

We are almost to the gig—I'll talk to you about this later. I'm reminded of a joke. . . .

This guy was in Alaska driving through the snow when his four-wheeler broke down. He left it with a mechanic while he went to get a sandwich. When he returned, the mechanic said, "Well, it looks like you blew a seal."

The guy replied, "Nope, just a little mayonnaise on my lip."

✳ March 16

TODAY IS FRIDAY, so it must be Billy Bob's. We are about an hour out of Fort Worth. Last night in Victoria was fun. Horace Logan, my old friend, came by. At one time Horace was one of the most powerful DJs in America as far as country music goes. KWKH in Shreveport, Louisiana, was the hot spot back then, and Horace ran the *Louisiana Hayride,* a very popular country music show. KWKH became one of the first fifty-thousand clear-channel watts that would reach all of America and beyond.

The difference between the *Grand Ole Opry* and the *Louisiana Hayride,* according to Horace, was the *Grand Ole Opry* would only hire known acts while the *Hayride* was known for discovering new talents. Hank Williams, Lefty Frizzell, Jim Reeves, Webb Pierce, and Faron Young were all members of the *Hayride* at one time.

In the late '50s, after the *Hayride,* Horace went to Dallas and ran the *Big D Jamboree,* another popular country music show at the time. That's where I first met him.

Horace is looking good for an old guy! He always told me to keep trying because he thought I was a little different. Different enough to have a chance to make it. I always appreciated his effort and admired his talent, as an MC and a country music professor. His knowledge of the record business and his ability to speak about it with dignity and class made him one of the greatest. A bunch of us owe a lot to Horace Logan.

One of my favorite stories of his he used to tell was about a young singer-songwriter trying to get on the *Louisiana Hayride.* They would hold auditions on Friday night for the Saturday night *Hayride* show. This guy came in looking kind of poor and scared. Horace listened to the guy and told him he thought he had talent, but that in order to get on the *Hayride,* it would help to have a record out, and he should try and improve his appearance a little, but please come back and try again.

The next Friday, the guy came back with a box of records he had made himself and a cowboy suit that Horace said also looked hand-made. Horace said, "OK, come back tomorrow night for the show." Saturday night came and Horace introduced the guy onstage, told the whole story to the audience how he came in first and he told him to come back with a record. In the meantime, the poor guy is backstage waiting and waiting, getting more and more nervous, and by the time Horace said, "and here he is," the guy was so scared that he ran out onto the stage with his guitar, hand-made Nudie suit, and an armful of records. The first thing he did was start throwing his records out into the audience, one at a time. Folks were ducking and dodging the flying records, trying to avoid decapitation. Horace never did say what happened to the guy.

I lived in the Portland, Oregon/Vancouver, Canada/Washington State area for awhile in the mid '50s when I was a disc jockey at radio station KVAN. My mother had moved to that area, and I followed. I

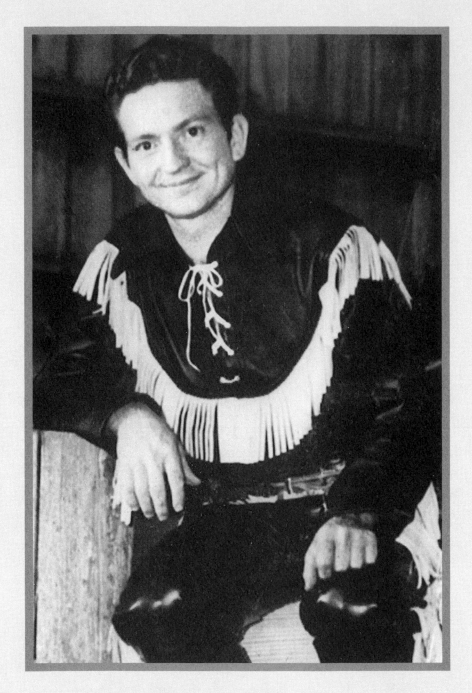

In costume for KVAN Radio,
Vancouver, Washington, 1956

really loved it there. "Cactus" Ken DeBorg, Shorty the Hired Hand, and all the folks at KVAN were great. I still miss them all.

Just before I went to Vancouver, I was working for KCNC in Fort Worth. I had a daily children's show from 1:00 P.M. to 2:00 P.M. as the kids got ready for their naps. Every day I played "The Red Headed Stranger." Written by Carl Stutz and Edith Lindeman, and sung by Arthur "Guitar Boogie" Smith, this was by far my most requested song. I'd start off the show every day, "This is your old cotton-pickin', snuff-dippin', tobaccer-chewin', stump-jumpin', gravy-soppin', coffee-pot-dodgin', dumplin'-eatin', frog-giggin' hillbilly from Hill County, Willie Nelson."

Who'll Buy My Memories?

A past that's sprinkled with the blues
A few old dreams that I can't use
Who'll buy my memories
Of things that used to be?
There were the smiles before the tears
And with the smiles some better years
Who'll buy my memories
Of things that used to be?

When I remember how things were
My memories all lead to her
I'd like to start my life anew
But memories just make me blue

A cottage small just built for two
A garden wall with violets blue
Who'll buy my memories
Of things that used to be?

There are so many important things to talk about, I wish I knew where to start. In Abbott we say, "I'm just like a duck. If it doesn't rain, I'll walk," and "A hard head makes a sore ass."

Our motto in Abbott was, and still is, "A winner never quits, and a quitter never wins." This was written above our black panther logo in the school gym. I saw it every day. It must have stuck. I believe that you can't lose if you don't give up. Even if you die, you'll die fighting. I remember one of the Rankin boys saying one day in a basketball game between Abbott and Byrum—someone offended him in some way—he jumped out in the middle of the gym and said, "My mama didn't raise nothin' but fighting kids!" I thought, "What a nice family."

The Abbott motto has carried me around the world several times, and helped me through a lot of interesting situations. Like when I first came to Houston. I hit town with my wife, Martha, and daughters, Lana, age four, and Susie, two. I was looking for a place to stay and I needed rent money, so I began to search for a place to play. I found a little place in Pasadena and got a job at the Esquire Ballroom, all the way across Houston, about an hour drive on the Hempstead highway.

It was a Monday afternoon, about three o'clock. Larry Butler and his band were rehearsing at the Esquire. I walked in, sat at a table, and waited until Larry took a break. I introduced myself and asked Larry if he wanted to buy any songs—ten dollars apiece. I sang them "I Gotta Get Drunk" and "Family Bible." He said, "Those songs are worth more than ten dollars, but I'll loan you the money to pay your rent, and I'll give you a job in my band." Thanks, Larry Butler.

Family Bible

There's a family Bible on the table
Its pages worn and hard to read
But the family Bible on the table
Will ever be my key to memories

At the end of the day when work was over
And when the evening meal was done
Dad would read to us from the family Bible
And we'd count our many blessings one by one

I can see us sitting 'round the table
When from the family Bible Dad would read
And I can hear my mother softly singing
Rock of Ages, Rock of Ages, cleft for me

Now this old world of ours is filled with trouble
This old world would oh so better be
If we found more Bibles on the table
And mothers singing Rock of Ages, cleft for me

I can see us sitting 'round the table
When from the family Bible Dad would read
And I can hear my mother softly singing
Rock of Ages, Rock of Ages, cleft for me

ONE NIGHT, LARRY was left in charge of the club while the owner, Raymond Prosky, went somewhere. Everything was fine until some

Left to right: Susie, Billy, Martha, and Lana

Me and Ed Knapps

drunk started giving the waitress trouble. Larry came off the bandstand to straighten things out. Naturally I had to help. When the dust cleared, Larry had his teeth knocked out and I had two broken ribs. Thanks, Larry, we're even. Just joking, I owe you a lot more than that.

I Gotta Get Drunk

Well, I gotta get drunk and I sure do dread it
*   'Cause I know just what I'm gonna do*
I'll start to spend my money
*   Calling everybody honey*
*   And wind up singing the blues*
I'll spend my whole paycheck on some old wreck
*   And brother, I can name you a few*
Well, I gotta get drunk and I sure do dread it
*   'Cause I know just what I'm gonna do*

Well I gotta get drunk, I can't stay sober
*   There's a lot of good people in town*
Who like to hear me holler
*   See me spend my dollars*
*   And I wouldn't think of letting them down*
There's a lot of good doctors that tell me
*   That I'd better start slowing it down*
But there's more old drunks
*   Than there are old doctors*
*   So I guess we'd better have another round*

———

I REMEMBER WORKING FOR a radio station in Pasadena, Texas, the year before I went to Nashville, at KRCT. I was on the air from 6:00 A.M. to . . . something. I forgot exactly. I was playing clubs around Houston every night from eight to midnight or later—so by the time I got home it was pretty late. I finally got fired for showing up late. I was making about fifteen dollars a night playing in different bands around town. One band-leader was Lucky Carlyle. I had been hiring myself out as a lead-guitar player and singer for Lucky.

After I went to work at the radio station, I started charging twenty-five dollars a night, because since I was a DJ, I could say where I'd be playing around town. I figured the free radio spot was worth another ten dollars a night. So when Lucky called for me to play, I asked, "How much does it pay, Lucky?"

He said, "Oh, fifteen dollars a night."

I said, "Well, I don't usually like to leave the house for less than twenty-five dollars."

Lucky said, "I'll bet you stay home a lot."

I thought about it. "You're right. I'll see you tonight."

I decided the steady fifteen dollars was better.

Night Life

When the evening sun goes down
You will find me hanging 'round
The night life
Ain't no good life
But it's my life

Many people just like me
Dreaming of old used-to-bes
   The night life
   Ain't no good life
   But it's my life

Listen to the blues that they're playing
Listen to what the blues are saying

Mine is just another scene
From the world of broken dreams
   The night life
   Ain't no good life
   But it's my life

I SOLD THE SONG "Family Bible" to Paul Buskirk, Claude Grey, and Walt Breeland for enough money to pay the rent. I also sold "Night Life" to the same three friends. I still thank them for the fifty dollars for "Family Bible" and the hundred dollars for "Night Life." I don't have any regrets about selling those songs. At the time I really needed the money. A hundred and fifty dollars in those days, and in my position, was like ten thousand dollars to me.

Larry Butler gave me a job playing in his band. Paul Buskirk gave me a job in his music studio, where I taught guitar and sold guitars and pianos. Paul Buskirk taught me how to read music, and I stayed a lesson or two ahead of my students. Every now and then I would hit a couple of good blues licks, or jump into "Under the Double Eagle," just to impress the little rascals.

We played out of a great teaching book called *Mel Bay Part 1:*

Teaching Little Fingers to Play. I recommend it highly to little fingers around the world.

The Storm Has Just Begun

Each night the raging storm clouds
    Take away the moon above
And each day the same clouds
    Take away the sun
My world is filled with darkness
And I'm lost without your love
And I realize the storm has just begun

Can't you see the lightning flashing
    Can't you hear the thunder roll
She's gone, she's gone
    The damage has been done
There's a storm within my heart
That keeps me crying night and day
And I realize the storm has just begun

The sun was shining brightly
    On the day that we were wed
The day God made the two of us as one
But since the day you left me,
    Storm clouds gather overhead
And I realize the storm has just begun

I don't want your help or pity
          I don't need your sympathy
All I want is you to be my only one
Another night is coming
          And a long night it will be
And I realize the storm has just begun

Billy Walker cut this song in the late '50s. It was one of the first songs I ever had recorded. He called it "The Storm Within My Heart."

Tonight I talked to Bill Mack, another great radio personality, who's been around as long as I have. He knows more about country music than most people, and he's still doing it. In fact, he can now be heard on satellite radio all over the world. He's another hero of mine who always fought for the things he believed in. God bless you, Bill Mack.

I was telling the Roger Miller joke to Bill about the guy in the used car lot kicking the tires of one of the cars. The salesman came up and said, "You thinking about buying a car?"

The guy said, "No, I'm going to buy a car. I was thinking about pussy."

Oh well, if my friends hadn't said so many funny things, this would be a short book.

These guys were in a bar. This one guy looks up and sees another guy at the end of the bar that looks a little like Jesus. He says, "Hey, that looks like Jesus!" His friends say, "He's crazy, that's not Jesus." The guy goes up to the one who looks like Jesus and says, "Hey, what's your name?"

"Jesus," the man replied. The guy said, "No you're not!"

Jesus said, "Yes I am."

"If you're really Jesus, cure my headache."

Jesus put his hand on the guy's head and the headache was cured. He called to his buddies to come on down, this is really Jesus. The second guy steps up and says, "If you're really Jesus, heal my back problem I've had since birth."

Jesus touches him on the back and the guy screams, "He's Jesus! I'm cured!"

So the two guys wave to the third guy. "Come on! It's really Jesus!"

The third guy comes running up and says, "Don't touch me. I'm getting one hundred percent disability."

BILLY BOB'S WAS A BLAST with lots of cowboys and cowgirls. It was good to see Joey and Jill Floyd tonight. They are such good musicians. We're on our way to Austin now to do a radio show at 1:00 P.M., a photo session at 3:00 P.M., and a show at the Austin Rodeo later tonight. Austin is home. There'll be a lot of mine and Poodie's friends there I'm sure.

> If we're backing up it's just to get a running start
> 'Cause everything we do we do with all our hearts
> And it don't really matter what they say
> We wouldn't have it any other way

Excuse me, sometimes I just break into song.

> We play our songs and play on our old guitars
> And it doesn't really matter where we are
> We wake up in a new world every day

And we wouldn't have it any other way
When it's time for us to move along
To a place we sometimes sing of in our songs
Raise your glasses high on that fine day
'Cause we wouldn't have it any other way

You know what you get when you cross a donkey with an onion? You get a piece of ass that'll bring a tear to your eye. You see, that's another Abbott joke.

My friend Casey Tibbs, World Champion All-Around Cowboy, had one of the neatest deals I had ever heard of. He was going to breed and raise cats. Then he was going to raise rats to feed to the cats, skin the cats, and sell the cat skins. He would feed the dead cats to the rats, and the rats to the cats, eliminating the need for food in both cat and rat. He would then cross the cat with a snake, and the cat would shed its skin *twice* a year, doubling the profits. Sadly, Casey died before his dream came true.

Ben Dorcy, the world's oldest band boy, was with us this trip. We are within his radius. Ben has worked for John Wayne, Ann-Margret, Buck Owens, Hank Thompson, Ray Price, and more recently, Robert Earl Keen, Pat Green, and Corey Morrow. He's one hard-working man. I told him tonight that he was insured by the company I've formed, with a two-dollar deductible. He wants a fifty-dollar deductible.

We said, "Only if you pay the fifty up front. We take no chances."

Ben said, "OK, it sounded like a better policy."

One time, when Ben was working in Nashville, he was walking in front of the Ryman Auditorium wearing a Nudie suit given to him by Hank Thompson. Somebody thought Ben was a star, and came up to him and said, "How do you get started in this business?"

Ben said, "There ain't but one way, hoss. You start at the bottom and go right to the top. Don't mess with that in-between shit."

Valentine

Valentine
Won't you be my valentine
Introduce your heart to mine
And be my valentine

Summertime
We could run and play like summertime
With storybooks and nursery rhymes
So be my valentine

Candy heart
If anyone could, you could have a candy heart
You're the sweetest of all sweethearts
Won't you give your heart to me?

Can't you see
I love you valentine
Won't you be my valentine
And won't you share your space with mine
Be my valentine

Candy heart
If anyone could, you could have a candy heart
You're the sweetest of all sweethearts
Won't you give your heart to me?
Can't you see
I love you, valentine

Won't you be my valentine
Introduce your heart to mine
      Be my valentine

Let me take the opportunity to talk for a few moments about my family—Lana, Susie, Billy, Paula, Amy, Lukas, and Micah. Everyone is so different. Everyone is definitely a free spirit, lovers of life, all with a great outlook on life, and I am so proud of them all that I could never put it into words.

Billy left us a while back, but I still think of him all the time and he is always with me.

"Don't stand at my grave and cry. I am not there.
I did not die."

—WRITER UNKNOWN

These are difficult times
These are difficult times
Lord, please give me a sign
For these are difficult times

My son Billy

Too Sick to Pray

I've been too sick to pray, Lord
That's why we ain't talked in awhile
It's been some of those days, Lord
I thought I was on my last mile
But I'm feeling OK, Lord
I never needed you more
I would have called you before
But I've been too sick to pray

Remember the family, Lord
I know they will remember you
In all of their prayers, Lord
They talk to you just like I do
Well I reckon that's all, Lord
That's all I can think of to say
And thank you, my friend
We'll be talking again
If I'm not too sick to pray

Remember the Good Times

Remember the good times
        They're smaller in number
        And easier to recall

Don't spend too much time on the bad times
Their staggering number will be
Heavy as lead on your mind

Don't waste a moment unhappy
Invaluable moments gone
With the leakage of time
As we leave on our own separate journeys
Moving west with the sun
To a place buried deep in our minds

Remember the good times

✴ *Sunday, March 18*

LAST NIGHT'S AUSTIN RODEO show was fun, with a sell-out crowd of thousands of happy rodeo and music lovers. Today I do a photo session, and then a recording session with Gillian Welch. Gillian is a fine writer and singer, and her song will be featured in the upcoming movie *The Journeyman.*

I played a part in the movie and was glad to sing any song with Gillian. Her latest recording of "I'll Fly Away" with Alison Krauss is one of the best renditions I've ever heard.

Now that the shows are over for a few days, I plan to enjoy time with my family. The bus is empty except for me. It sure is quiet. There's a movie playing on TV called *Dream West.* It's good, but it's the longest son of a bitch I think I can remember.

Here's a song me and Bob Dylan wrote for Farm Aid.

Heartland

There's a home place under fire tonight
      In the heartland
And the bankers are taking
      My home and my land from me
There's a big aching hole in my chest now
      Where my heart was
And a hole in the sky where God used to be

There's a home place under fire tonight
      In the heartland
There's a well with water so bitter nobody can drink
Ain't no way to get high, and my mouth is so dry
      That I can't speak
Don't they know that I'm dying?
      Why's nobody crying for me?

My American dream
Fell apart at the seams
You tell me what it means
You tell me what it means

There's a home place under fire tonight
      In the heartland
The bankers are taking my home and my land away

There's a young boy closing his eyes tonight
In the heartland
Who will wake up a man with a home and a loan
He can't pay

His American dream
Fell apart at the seams
You tell me what it means
You tell me what it means

My American dream
Fell apart at the seams
You tell me what it means
You tell me what it means

There's a home place under fire tonight
In the heartland

FARM AID WILL HAPPEN IN INDIANA on September 29, 2001. I hope it all goes well. I'm sure it will. It's in the middle of the farm belt and John Mellencamp's home state. It will be possible to show the Capitol Hill crowd that there are still some of us who believe in the small family farmer, the first rung on the economic ladder. When you see things going wrong in a country, the first thing you should do is look at how family farmers are treated. How are we treating the first rung on our ladder? Because when the backbone of our country is broken and the first rung on the ladder is weakened, everything collapses. We all come crashing down. You can cut taxes all you want. You can do everything in this

world for every other rung on the ladder. But when the family farmer goes under, it's just a matter of time before everyone else follows.

We had well over eight million small family farmers, and now we're down to two million, losing three hundred to five hundred a week. If we don't get a farm bill, a good one, there will be no more small family farmers left. Farm Aid will help all we can, because someone has to repair that bottom rung of the ladder, and time is of the essence. The reason every civilization has gone under in the past was because of an inability to feed its people. We are running out of time.

Speaking of time, there was a man standing in an orchard holding a pig by its hind legs. The farmer held the pig up and the pig would take the apples out of the trees with his mouth and drop them into a basket below. As soon as he picked one apple and dropped it into the basket, he would reach for another one. A man passing by stopped to watch. He said, "I'll bet it took a long time to teach that pig to do that!"

The guy said, "Oh, time don't mean nothing to a pig!"

Back to the farmer: Both Democrats and Republicans are going to have to agree in order to pass a new farm bill. The factory farms are the worst possible things we can do to the people, the environment, and the general health of everyone. We have already seen the dangers of disease in our livestock. Mad cow disease, foot-and-mouth disease—there are all kinds of diseases which, according to government reports, "may or may not be harmful to humans." Either way, it's easier for small family farmers to insure a healthier climate on the farm, because there are a few pigs on a few acres of ground, or a variety of products spread over several hundred acres—not a hundred thousand pigs in one big pigpen outside your retirement home in the country. The flies and smell from the waste is unbearable for miles. Just ask any of the people who live there. I daresay that there are no politicians living in those areas, or they would be screaming at the top of their lungs.

I hear politicians from both parties debating various issues on TV or radio talk shows—tax breaks for the wealthy, health benefits for the poor, social security benefits for the old, medicine and drug costs. *No one* mentions the family farmer. This is because there are millions and millions of dollars spent each year by big food conglomerates who want to keep things just the way they are. Hopefully someone with balls will come out against the money that keeps the farmer down. So far, the brave guys have been beaten back. Keep fighting! There are a lot of farmers and ranchers who need your help.

✳

FIVE POINT AGENDA FOR SAVING FAMILY FARMERS AND RECLAIMING RURAL AMERICA

1. **Pass a farm bill that will restore a fair price for farmers:**
   - Establish price supports to ensure that farm income comes from the marketplace and not from taxpayers.
   - Create a farmer-owned reserve to ensure food security in times of scarcity and price stability in times of plenty.
   - Avoid wasteful overproduction through inventory management.
   - Maintain planting flexibility.
   - Establish national dairy policy to ensure a farmer's cost of production plus a return on investment.
2. **Restore competition through strict enforcement of antitrust law.**
   - Place a moratorium on mergers and acquisitions in agribusiness, transportation, food processing, manufacturing, and retail companies.

- Require strict enforcement of the Packers and Stock-yards Act to end price discrimination.
- Enact a ban on packer ownership of livestock.

3. **Protect consumers and the environment.**
- Require labeling of meat and other foods imported into the U.S. to give consumers the right to know and choose the country of origin of their food.
- Stop the expansion of large-scale factory farms.
- Protect environmentally fragile lands and habitats.

4. **Eliminate industry subsidies paid by independent producers.**
- Hold referenda on the mandatory pork and beef check-offs as petitioned by independent producers to break up corporate control of livestock.
- Oppose governmental nominations that represent the interests of corporate agriculture.

5. **Negotiate fair trade agreements.**
- Ensure that all countries retain the right to develop farm programs that respond to the needs of their farmers and consumers.
- Put an end to export dumping (the sale of commodities below the cost of production), which undermines our domestic economy.
- Ensure that environmental protection, fair wages, and workers rights are part of every trade agreement.

This lady was driving through the country and saw a man making love to a sheep out behind the barn. She drove into town and reported the incident to the police. At the trial, the judge said, "OK, lady. Exactly what did you see?"

The lady said, "Your honor, I was driving down this country road and I saw a man making love to a sheep. You're not going to believe this part. When they were through making love, the sheep curled up next to the guy, put its head on the guy's shoulder, and just went to sleep."

One guy on the jury leaned over to another juror and whispered, "Yeah, they'll do that!"

ANOTHER THING THAT I'M DEFINITELY AGAINST are the genetically altered foods they are trying to shove down our throats. Something wrong is going on. Fortunately, the American public is demanding more and more organic foods. They want a tomato to taste like a tomato instead of having no taste at all. More people remember the difference and are insisting on better quality foods for their families. As more and more people are offered a choice between organic and pesticide-filled non-organic foods, they are choosing the healthier organic foods.

IT'S 1:30 IN the morning, March 19.

I believe I'll have an organic hit and hit the hay. 'Nite all.

✴ *Wednesday, March 21*

DR. RED DUKE IS ONE OF the best doctors I know, if not the best. He came from the same part of Texas I did, where a hard head makes a sore ass and the truth shall set you free. Red is one of the best friends I have, and he is by far the best friend a sick picker can have. Just this year he has saved the lives of two of my best picker friends. I won't mention their names in case they write a hot check for the hospital bill.

Dr. Duke was the doctor who had treated my mother before she died. Dr. Duke was at the funeral. Later, my father-in-law went to him with lung cancer. He died. Dr. Duke was at that funeral. After the funeral, I jokingly said to Dr. Duke, "If you don't quit losing them I'm going to quit sending them to you."

He looked at me with that Hill County grin and said, "Willie, you're just going to have to get them to me earlier."

Red was telling me today about the new Red Ass Salve. Just as you start to feel the symptoms, rub a little on the affected area. If irritation persists, and you find yourself in the advanced stages, you should stick the whole jar up your ass.

I heard one of the band members say the other day that his wife was using some kind of cream on her breasts to make them bigger. He told her, "Use some toilet paper. Look what it's done for your ass!"

The picker shall remain nameless for security reasons.

THE GUY WOKE UP next to this strange girl and said, "You don't have AIDS, do you?" She said no. Then he said, "Good. I can't afford to catch that shit again!"

THE FATHER WAS RESISTING being put into a nursing home. After hours of arguing, he was finally persuaded to go. The first day he called and said, "Thank you, son. I can't tell you how much I love it here. Thank you for talking me into it."

The son said, "Well, what happened?"

He said, "This morning a beautiful nurse came in, bathed me all over, and then gave me the best head I have ever had. Son, it's just heaven! Thanks again."

Me and Paul

The next day, the father was back on the phone. "Son, you've got to get me out of here."

"Why Dad?"

"Son, I was walking down the hallway to the bathroom and I fell down. This big guy jumped on me and screwed me in the ass for an hour."

"Well, Dad. Remember all the fun you had yesterday?"

The dad said, "Son, I just get a hard-on every now and then, but I fall down two or three times a day!"

Me and Paul

It's been rough and rocky traveling
But I'm finally standing upright on the ground
After taking several readings
I'm surprised to find my mind's still fairly sound
I guess Nashville was the roughest
But I know I've said the same about them all
    We received our education
    In the cities of the nation
    Me and Paul

Almost busted in Laredo
But for reasons that I'd rather not disclose
But if you're staying in a motel there and leave
Just don't leave nothing in your clothes
And at the airport in Milwaukee
They refused to let us board the plane at all

They said we looked suspicious
But I believe they like to pick on
Me and Paul

On a package show in Buffalo
With us and Kitty Wells and Charley Pride
The show was long and we're just sitting there
And we'd come to play and not just for the ride
Well, we drank a lot of whiskey
So I don't know if we went on that night at all
I don't think they even missed us
I guess Buffalo ain't geared for
Me and Paul

CUT TO THIRTY YEARS LATER . . .

✳

✳ *Saturday, April 7*

Buffalo, New York, was sort of cold and rainy, but the crowd was warm and receptive. We played more than two hours. The sound in the theater was so good. Sister Bobbie thought everything sounded good, and she has a good ear for that kind of thing.

John Rosenfelder from Island Records came by with some friends. Later, Heidi Raphael, Mickey's beautiful wife, came by the bus with some of her relatives. They are just as nice as she is.

I saw some of the video footage that David Anderson shot tonight.

Some of the shots from the back let me know that I have some more running to do.

We just left Nashville where I went into the studio and recorded a Bernie Taupin–Matt Serletic song called "Mendocino County Line." Lee Ann Womack sang with me. She is a fellow Texan, from east Texas, I think around Jacksonville. She sings wonderful. I was proud to sing with her. The song will be on my new CD, *The Great Divide*, due to be released on Island in a few months.

Sheryl Crow, Rob Thomas, Kid Rock, Bonnie Raitt, Brian McKnight, Lee Ann Womack, the Jordanaires, Alison Krauss, the Waters Family, and a great band lent their talent on *The Great Divide*. Thanks to you *all*.

The Great Divide

Here we are, standing where the highways cross
Here we are, saying goodbye
Here we are acting like two crazy kids
We've come too far, to ever see it end like this
Just another love lost in the great divide

Remember how we used to dance together
Remember how I used to hold you tight
You ask me if I'd leave and I said never
And that's still right

Summer sun, no prettier than summer rain
Some are gone, and some are coming back again
Other loves, lost in the great divide

Herky Williams, my longtime friend and ASCAP rep in Nashville; my manager, Mark Rothbaum; Steve Hauser, a booking agent from William Morris; and I played a round of golf yesterday at Herky's home course, the Old Natchez Trail, a beautiful golf course outside of Nashville. The weather cooperated, and we all played just bad enough to stay friends.

That reminds me of a joke. . . .

There were a bunch of policemen standing around a woman's body out in the center of the fairway at the local country club. A lone golfer was standing with his driver in his hand. The policeman asked what happened. "Well, officer," the guy said, "I didn't see her. I swear I didn't see her! I hit a shot right down the middle and it hit her in the head. I really did not see her."

One officer said, "Well, sir. That explains the ball to the head. But what about that other one we found in her rectum?"

The guy said, "Oh, yes. That was my mulligan."

> *It was just an old Titleist 2*
> *But it did what it intended to do*
> *We met in the fairway, balled in the stairway*
> *Thanks to the old Titleist 2*

The blonde went into the body shop to get a couple of dents fixed in her car. The guy at the body shop decided to play a joke on the blonde. He said, "You can save a lot of money if you want to. Blow on the exhaust pipe and all the dents will come out of your car." The blonde said, "Thanks, I'll try that!"

She went home, parked in the driveway, crawled under the car, and

started blowing on the exhaust pipe. She was blowing and blowing when her friend, another blonde, came over and said, "What in the hell are you doing?"

The first blonde said, "I'm trying to blow the dents out of my car."

Her friend said, "Duh! You've gotta roll up the windows!"

LEAVING HOUSTON AND going to Nashville was not really a hard choice for me. It was time. I had a hit song. "Family Bible" was #1 in the charts, and my 1941 Buick had just about enough life left in it to get me there—maybe. It actually made the trip without a problem. However, it did immediately settle into the earth forever after it delivered me safely to Nashville. May it forever rest in peace.

I wrote this song on that first trip to Nashville. . . .

I'm Gonna Lose a Lot of Teardrops

I'm going 'round in circles
 Acting like a fool
I played the game of love
 And I don't even know the rules
I gave my heart to someone
 She broke it just today
And I'm gonna lose a lot of teardrops this way

I suppose I should be careful
 But how was I to know

She looked so sweet and innocent
But that's the way it goes
It happens to the best of us
At least that's what they say
But I'm gonna lose a lot of teardrops this way

Something sure had better change
But what am I to do
Surely there's someone around
Who needs a love that's true
But I guess I'll keep on searching
But one thing I can say
I'm gonna lose a lot of teardrops this way

Touch Me

Touch me
Touch the hand of the man
Who once owned all the world
Touch me
Touch the arms that once held
All the charms of the world's sweetest girl
Touch me
Maybe someday you may need
To know how it feels when you lose
So touch me
Then you'll know
How it feels when you lose

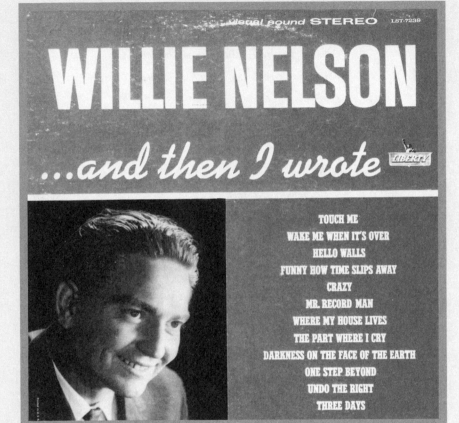

visual sound STEREO   LST-7239

WILLIE NELSON

...and then I wrote   LIBERTY

TOUCH ME

WAKE ME WHEN IT'S OVER

HELLO WALLS

FUNNY HOW TIME SLIPS AWAY

CRAZY

MR. RECORD MAN

WHERE MY HOUSE LIVES

THE PART WHERE I CRY

DARKNESS ON THE FACE OF THE EARTH

ONE STEP BEYOND

UNDO THE RIGHT

THREE DAYS

My first album

Watch me
> *Watch the eyes that have seen*
> *All the heartache and pain in the land*

And be thankful
> *That you're happy, though standing*
> *So close to the world's bluest man*

Don't forget me
> *Take a good look at someone who's lost*
> *Everything he can lose*

And touch me
> *Then you'll know*
> *How you feel with the blues*

Crazy

Crazy
> *Crazy for feeling so lonely*

I'm crazy
> *Crazy for feeling so blue*

I knew
> *You'd love me as long as you wanted*

And then someday

You'd leave me for somebody new

Worry
> *Why do I let myself worry?*

Wondering
> *What in the world did I do*

Crazy
> *For thinking that my love could hold you*
I'm crazy for trying
Crazy for crying
And I'm crazy
> *For loving you*

The Part Where I Cry

Life is a picture in which I play the lead
But my biggest line was goodbye
Now my leading lady has walked out on me
And this is the part where I cry

I was great in the scene
> *Where she found someone new*
You should have seen my look of surprise
And if you have just walked into the picture
This is the part where I cry

And after the picture is over
And it's judged for the part where she lied
The award of achievement that's given
Will be mine for the part where I cry

Wake Me When It's Over

I'm getting tired now
I gotta get some sleep now
I guess I've been worried much too long
And don't wake me till it's over
  When the need for you is gone

I was so happy before I loved you
I want to be like I was before
So don't wake me till it's over
  When I won't want you anymore

My eyes are getting weak now
Gotta get some sleep now
I gotta rest my aching head
I just wanna lay here
Just let me stay here
  Till the blues get up
  And leave my bed

Good night, darling
Good night, darling
Good night forevermore
And don't wake me till it's over
  When I won't want you anymore

My eyes are getting weak now
I gotta get some sleep now

I gotta rest my aching head
Just let me lay here
Let me stay here
  Till the blues get up
  And leave my bed

Good night darling
Good night darling
Good night forevermore
And don't wake me till it's over
  When I won't want you anymore

Three Days

There are three days I know that I'll be blue
Three days that I'll always dream of you
And it does no good to wish these days would end
'Cause these same three days start over again

Three days that I dread to see arrive
Three days that I hate to be alive
Three days filled with tears and sorrow
  Yesterday, today, and tomorrow

This song was inspired by a joke I had heard. A drunk walked up to a guy on the street and said, "I ain't eaten in three days. Yesterday, today, and tomorrow."

One Step Beyond

I'm just one step before losing you
And I'm just one step ahead of the blues
But I know that there's been pain and misery
Long before this old world ever heard of me

And I know it will hurt to see you go
But we'll just add one more heartache to the score
And though I still love you as before
I'm just one step beyond caring anymore

Bet that you're surprised that I could feel this way
After staying home and waiting night and day
For someone who cared so much for me
You'd come home just long enough to laugh at me

I don't know just when my feelings changed
I just know I could never feel the same
And though I still love you as before
I'm just one step beyond caring anymore

Darkness on the Face of the Earth

The morning that you left me
Was just another day
How could I see the sorrow that had found me?
And then you laughed and told me

That I was in your way
And I turned and ran as heaven fell around me

I stumbled through the darkness
My footsteps were unsure
I lived within a world that had no sunshine
When you left me darling
My world came to an end
And there was darkness on the face of the earth

The stars fell out of heaven
The moon could not be found
The sun was in a million pieces
  Scattered all around
Why did you ever leave me?
You knew how it would hurt
And now there's darkness on the face of the earth

Where My House Lives

Stop here, across the street to your right
  That's where my house lives
Sometimes I stayed there at night
But mostly I was on the move
Business first, you know
And she'd wait there in her lonely room
But oh, that's been so long ago
  She's gone now

She couldn't stand to be alone
And now it waits there
This house that used to be my home

I never go there 'cause it holds too many memories
Since she's gone
But right there is where my house
Lives all alone

HARLAN HOWARD, my old songwriting buddy, once said, "If I ever think about getting married again, I'm just gonna find some gal that I don't like too much and buy her a house."

Misery Mansion

Misery mansion
So cold and so gray
You look so lonely
Since she went away

Misery mansion
What secrets you hide
Of a love
That has faded and died

You know all the reasons
Why she said goodbye

And you stand there in silence
While I sit and cry

Misery mansion
Oh, how you've changed
Your walls hold the sorrow
That loneliness brings
A love of a lifetime
Forever is gone
Misery mansion, my home

Home Motel

What used to be my home has changed
To just a place to stay
A crumbling last resort when day is through
Sometimes between sundown and dawn
Somehow I find my way
To this home motel
On Lost Love Avenue

No one seems to really care
If I come here at all
And the one who seems to care the least is you
I'm gonna hang a neon sign
With letters big and blue
Home Motel
On Lost Love Avenue

No one seems to really care
    If I come here at all
And the one who seems to care the least is you
I'm gonna hang a neon sign
With letters big and blue
    Home Motel
    On Lost Love Avenue

Lonely Little Mansion

I'm a lonely little mansion for sale
Furnished with everything but love

I'm looking for someone
    To come live in me
I've got a large picture window
    And a yard filled with trees
The sign reads "two stories"
And that's all that's for sale
But there's so many stories
    I could tell

My windows are closed
And I'm gasping for air
My carpets are spotted
With tear stains here and there
A torn photograph still lies on my floor
And two sweethearts don't live here anymore

I'm a lonely little mansion for sale
And for someone I'd fit just like a glove
I'm a lonely little mansion for sale
Furnished with everything but love

I Just Stopped By

I just stopped by to see the house I used to live in
I hope that you don't mind
I won't stay very long
So long ago someone and I lived here together
And then so suddenly I found myself alone

I couldn't stand the thought
Of living here without her
And so I moved away to let my memories die
But my memories outlived my better judgment
This may sound strange to you
But I just thought I'd stop by

The very door you're standing in
She used to stand there
And wait for me to come home every night
And when I'd see her standing there
I'd run to meet her
These things were on my mind
So I just thought I'd stop by

I guess that I should leave
Someone just might not understand
And I'm aware of how the neighbors like to pry
But you can tell them all today
A most unhappy man
Was in the neighborhood
And he just thought he'd stop by

HARLAN HOWARD, ROGER MILLER, AND I used to have a lot of fun together at the BMI Awards dinners in Nashville. We would sit right down front, drink white Russians, and run Frances Preston crazy. As Nashville's head of BMI, it was her job to try and make everyone happy. God bless her. She did it better than anybody. Every time an award was announced, Harlan, Roger, and I would all three jump up and accept it. By the time the real winner got to the podium, things were a bit confusing. Frances smiled through the whole thing. She was the best, she's a treasure. I love you, Frances. You put up with a lot between me, Harlan, Roger, and Hank Cochran.

By the way, Hank was responsible for me signing with Pamper Music in the early '60s. Instead of taking his fifty-dollar-a-week raise in salary as a writer, he convinced Pamper Music to give it to me. It was then I felt like a professional songwriter. Thanks, Hank.

I came to town with "Night Life," "Mr. Record Man," "Crazy," "Funny How Time Slips Away," and a few others. Hank had heard some of my songs one night at Tootsie's Orchid Lounge in Nashville. Everyone hung out at Tootsie's. She loved all the crazy people, Fluffo and Flutter Lips (better known as Wayne Walker and Mel Tillis), Faron Young, Hank, Charlie Dick (Patsy Cline's husband), Little Jimmy Dickens, and Billy Walker.

Tootsie

Billy Walker soon had a hit with "Funny How Time Slips Away." He had helped me out one time in Springfield, Missouri, and now again in Nashville. He is a real friend. A smart man once said if you go through life and make *one* real friend, you are a lucky person. T. Texas Tyler, another old buddy of mine, said that he was a man with a million friends—so I know I'm in there somewhere. I feel like I have a lot of real good friends.

Funny How Time Slips Away

Well, hello there
     My it's been a long, long time
How am I doin'?
     Oh, I guess that I'm doing fine
It's been so long now
But it seems like
     It was only yesterday
Gee, ain't it funny
How time slips away?

How's your new love?
     I hope that he's doing fine
I heard you told him
     That you'd love him till the end of time
Now, that's the same thing
     That you told me
     Seems like just the other day

Gee, ain't it funny
How time slips away?

Gotta go now
    I guess I'll see you around
Don't know when though
    Never know when I'll be back in town
But just remember
    What I tell you
    In time, you're gonna pay
And it's surprising
How time slips away

Mr. Record Man

Mr. Record Man, I'm looking for
    A song I heard today
There was someone blue singing about
    Someone who went away
Just like me his heart was yearning
    For a love that used to be
It's a lonely song about a lonely man, like me

I was driving down the highway
    With my radio turned on
And the man that I heard singing
    Seemed so blue and all alone

As I listened to his lonely song
I wondered could it be
Could there somewhere be another lonely man,
like me?

There was something about a love
That didn't treat him right
And he'd wake from troubled sleep
And cry her name at night
Mister Record Man, oh get this record for me
Won't you please
It's a lonely song about a lonely man, like me

SOME OF THE FUNNIEST STORIES to come out of Nashville are about Hank Snow, the "Singing Ranger." He was a huge country music star in the 1950s and '60s who was born in Canada. His first hit, "Brand on My Heart," was one of my all-time favorites.

Hank and I did an album together, one of the highlights of my life. Not only was he a gentleman, but he was an excellent example for young artists to try to follow.

His fiddle player, Chubby Wise, also a great musician, was Hank's right-hand man for years. One night, Hank was performing his show and the spotlight was in his eyes, and he got too close to the orchestra pit and fell in. He looked up and said, "Goddamn it, Chubby. Why don't you watch where I'm going?"

Once, Chubby stood up to take a fiddle course and got a little too close to Hank. His fiddle bow caught Hank's toupee, took it off, and sailed it out into the crowd. Hank kept singing, Chubby kept fiddling, and someone went home with Hank Snow's hair. Only in country music.

Nashville, 1961

Congratulations

I can tell that you're already growing tired of me
You want no part of me
Even started lying to me
And if you started out to break this heart inside of me
Congratulations to you, dear
You're doing fine

I pass you on the street and you don't speak to me
You just look at me
Then you walk away from me
If you started out to make a fool of me
Congratulations to you, dear
You're doing fine

Well, you should be commended for
The sorrow you caused me
How does it feel to be the queen of misery?
(So) if you started out
to break this heart inside of me
Congratulations to you, dear
You're doing fine

Hello Walls

Hello walls
       How'd things go for you today?
Don't you miss her
       Since she up and walked away?
And I'll bet you dread to spend
Another lonely night with me
But, lonely walls, I'll keep you company

Hello window
       Well, I see that you're still here
Aren't you lonely
       Since our darling disappeared?
Well, look here, is that a teardrop
In the corner of your pane?
Now, don't you try to tell me that it's rain

She went away
       And left us all alone
       The way she planned
Guess we'll have to learn to get along
       Without her if we can

Hello ceiling
       I'm gonna stare at you awhile
You know I can't sleep
       So won't you bear with me awhile?
We must all stick together
Or else I'll lose my mind

> *'Cause I've got a feeling*
> *She'll be gone a long, long time*

Years ago, Hank and Faron Young, another great character in country music, were on the same bill together. Over the years, they had never gotten along very well but found themselves backstage in a dressing room together, having a drink and telling jokes. Faron said, "Hank, here we are backstage having a great time drinking and joking together. Normally we wouldn't even speak to each other."

Hank said, "Oh, Faron. I'd say hello."

Faron Young was one of the first people I met when I got to Nashville. I met him at Tootsie's Orchid Lounge. I was jamming upstairs with Buddy Emmons and Jimmy Day (two of the greatest steel guitar players in the world), Hank Cochran, and a few more. Faron came in and I sang him a couple of my songs, "Congratulations" and "Hello Walls." He recorded them both. The record came out and was a huge hit.

Before the money started coming in, I was still broke, making a living playing bass on the road with Ray Price. A good job, but not much money. I saw Faron at Tootsie's and I offered to sell him all the rights to "Hello Walls" for five hundred dollars. He said, "You're crazy! That song has already sold more than that. Here's the five hundred. Pay me back when you have it."

He really did me a favor. Since then, "Hello Walls" has earned well more than a million dollars. Thank you, Faron.

My first royalty check was for twenty thousand dollars. When I finally got it, I found Faron at Tootsie's and immediately grabbed him around the neck and planted a big kiss on his mouth. I probably shouldn't say anything now that he's gone, but I think he liked it. I tried to pay him the five hundred dollars that I owed him, but he

Faron Young and me

wouldn't take it. I was raising calves at the time to try and sell, so Faron said, "Why don't you just give me one of those calves when you get him fattened up and we'll call it even."

The months went by, then the years. One day I saw Faron at Tootsie's again. He said, "That calf must weigh about six thousand pounds by now!"

We had a good laugh, but he still wouldn't let me pay him.

Many years later, I was playing the Austin Livestock Show and Rodeo. That night at the charity auction, my son Billy decided to bid on this registered Seminole bull. He wound up with the winning bid of seventeen thousand dollars. That was about seven thousand dollars more than I made that night. I couldn't give it back, it was a charity auction. I could write it off . . . right? Anyway, now I have a two-thousand-pound bull. What the hell am I going to do with it? My son Billy said, "Dad, we can make a killing in breeding fees!"

I said, "Right. But now I have to come up with seven thousand dollars just to get the son of a bitch home!"

Billy said, "Right."

Now I have to find a place to put him. I got an idea. I still owe Faron Young a fat calf, and this is one of the fattest he could ever get. So I had Bill Polk, the gentleman who worked for me and took care of the livestock, to load him up and take him to Nashville. He took him right to Faron's office and left him in the trailer, in the parking lot.

I called Faron and told him his calf was out front.

"What calf?"

"How soon we forget," I said. He called me back later to say thanks, and that this was the heaviest bull he'd ever seen. He said he was going to make a fortune in breeding fees. I thought, *Right. . . .*

———

PAMPER MUSIC WAS a company owned by Ray Price and Hal Smith. Hank Cochran and I were out behind the offices in a garage that had been turned into a sound studio and a place to write. There was no phone, one window, a piano, and a couple of guitars. Maedell Sandusky, the secretary, came in and told Hank he had a phone call. By the time Hank had gotten back from his call, I had written "Hello Walls." If Hank hadn't gotten that phone call we would have written it together and it would have been half his. We laughed a lot about the phone call that cost him half of "Hello Walls." I may have laughed a little more than Hank did.

We did write songs together though. One night we were in the basement of my house in Ridgetop. We wrote seven songs. One of them is called "What Can You Do to Me Now?" The next day my house burned down.

What Can You Do to Me Now?

> *What can you do to me now*
> *That you haven't done to me already?*
> *You broke my pride and made me cry out loud*
> *What can you do to me now?*
>
> *I'm seeing things that I never thought I'd see*
> *You've opened up the eyes inside of me*
> *How long have you been doing this to me?*
> *I'm seeing sides of me that I can't believe*

Someway, somehow, I'll make a man of me
I will build me back the way I used to be
Much stronger now, the second time around
　　　　'Cause what can you do to me now?

The Party's Over

Turn out the lights, the party's over
They say that all good things must end
Call it a night, the party's over
And tomorrow starts the same old thing again

What a crazy, crazy party
Never seen so many people
Laughing, dancing, look at you, you're having fun
But look at me, I'm almost crying
But that don't keep her love from dying
Misery, 'cause for me, the party's over

Once I had a love undying
I didn't keep it, wasn't trying
Life for me was just one party and then another
I broke her heart so many times
Had to have my party wine
Then one day she said
　　　　"Sweetheart, the party's over"

———

I WAS AT A CHRISTMAS PARTY AT Lucky Moeller's office. I get a phone call from my nephew Randy, who was at the house in Ridgetop. He said, "Uncle Willie, the house is burning."

I said, "Is everybody OK?" He said yes. I then said, "Pull the car in the garage and get out."

Sure enough, when I got there, it was burning pretty good. There were fire trucks, police cars, and a lot of other people. I ran in through the back door and the kitchen was full of smoke, firemen, policemen and I don't know who all. I walked down the hall to a closet, picked up my guitar and a bag of weed, and ran out the back door, giving the weed to a friend who ran to the woods and hid it.

Everyone had gotten out of the house OK and they put the fire out before it reached the garage. Too bad, too, it was a piece-of-shit car. I moved to Texas.

Texas

Listen to my song
And if you want to sing along
It's about where I belong
Texas

Sometime far into the night
And until the morning light
I pray with all my might
to be in
Texas

It's where I want to be
It's the only place for me
Where my spirit can be free
Texas

AFTER THE HOUSE BURNED IN RIDGETOP, I moved to Austin. I thought about Houston first because Connie's family lived there. But after visiting sister Bobbie in Austin, I decided this was a better spot for me. The weather was better, the hill country was beautiful, and the Austin music scene was well under way with Jerry Jeff Walker, Steve Fromholz, Michael Murphey, Gary P. Nunn, and just a lot of great fans.

I was playing Big G's in Round Rock, a cowboy/redneck good-ole-boy-and-girl beer joint. I saw a couple of long-haired cowboys in there. Very interesting, I thought. Then I went to the Armadillo World Headquarters, and there I met a lot of long-haired cowboys and cowgirls who liked to drink a beer and listen to country music. I saw two audiences in the same area, separated by what was called a generation gap. The old and the new coming together, or trying to come together. They were finding common ground, country music.

I called Waylon. I said, "Waylon, you're the luckiest son of a bitch alive just to know me. I'm gonna save your ass again. Come to Austin." And, of course, when the Armadillo crowd heard Waylon they loved him at first sight. They could relate. Here's another crazy, talented lost soul looking for new friends. And he found them. We both did. Long live Austin, Texas, the Armadillo World Headquarters, and, of course, Big G's, where the heart of two worlds came together.

———

WAYLON WROTE most of this song, but I took half.

Good-Hearted Woman

A long time forgotten
     Her dreams have just fell by the way
And the good life he promised
     Ain't what she's living today
But she never complains of the bad times
     Or the bad things he's done, Lord
She just talks about the good times they've had
     And all the good times to come

She's a good-hearted woman
     In love with a good-timing man
And she loves him in spite of his ways
     That she don't understand
Through teardrops and laughter
     They'll pass through this world hand in
        hand
This good-hearted woman
     In love with a good-timing man

He likes the night life, the bright lights
     And his good-timing friends
And when the party's all over
     She'll welcome him back home again

Lord knows she don't understand him
But she does the best that she can
She's a good-hearted woman
In love with a good-timing man

"Outlaws"

IN THE EARLY '70S, the name "Outlaw music" was given to some of us by Hazel Smith, a friend and writer in Nashville. I wanted Hazel to tell you in her own words how it happened. . . .

During '72 and '73, music by Willie, Waylon Jennings, and a bevy of cosmic creators began to find itself on the side of the majority. Hippies and lawyers, rednecks and suits, sat side by side on the Texas ground and dug Willie Nelson, Billy Joe Shaver, Jerry Jeff Walker, et al. It was unlike anything I had ever seen in the three decades I'd been in the music business.

In the beginning, radio sparsely programmed the music. Three stations had the balls to play only "Progressive music," as we called it for lack of a better term, and they were in Ashboro, North Carolina; Flint, Michigan; and Austin, Texas. Like western swing, rhythm and blues, and bluegrass, I knew the music needed a hook. "Progressive" was too uppity and prissy.

Searching out names for the genre, "Renegade" wasn't bad. But if you read Webster's, *you'll find it's not good. "Outlaw" crossed my mind time and again. Perhaps the Lee Clayton song, "Ladies Love Outlaws," was the inspiration. I can't say, but I can say I looked up "outlaw" in* Webster's Collegiate Dictionary, *and the one line that jumped out at me was, "Living on the outside of the written law."*

Outlaws and solid citizens (left to right): Ray Stevens,
Waylon Jennings, me, Bobby Bare, Glen Campbell, and
Ralph Emery in 1990 in Nashville.

Waylon frowned, Willie shrugged. Tompall Glaser said, "Don't tell nobody you named it." Truth is, those guys just wanted to pick, sing, and make a living. I'll tell you how great Outlaw music was. The creators are in the Country Music Hall of Fame. Enough said? Enough said.

—Hazel Smith

✳ *April 9, Williamsport, Pennsylvania, 9:30 P.M.*

I MADE A BIG RUSH TO GET TO my pen and paper to write something brilliant. Now I've forgotten it. Oh well. It couldn't have been that brilliant.

The other day a lady golfer came into the pro shop complaining of a terrible beesting. "Where did it sting you?" asked the golf pro. "Between the first and second hole," she cried. The pro said, "Well, the first thing, your stance is too wide!"

We had a great golf game today, me, Bee, Poodie, and Paul. We met a lot of nice people at the golf course. They made us feel right at home, and for four old guys, we didn't play too badly.

Scooter Franks came by the bus and we talked and laughed awhile. Scooter and his brother, Bo, have been handling the concessions on the road with me for many years. Scooter drives along behind the buses every night. He travels every mile we do, and does a terrific job of hawking swag. I let him read a little from this book today, and he laughed in all the right places. Thank you, Scooter.

I'VE BEEN WATCHING the stock market go up and down for several years. It's like "follow your bouncing money." I don't own any stock at this time, so I can watch and sing along. A lot of the guys in the band own stock, and it's interesting to see how they've aged. Paul English told me today that he has already lost half a million dollars in the stock market this year. I thought that was really bad, but I said, "Paul, you're the only drummer I know who can say that."

They all have that "leave it alone and it will be fine" attitude. I'm beginning to think they're right.

Did you hear about the nervous bank robber? He walked into the bank and yelled, "Stick up your ass or I'll blow your hands off!"

Paul Simon is on TV doing "Graceland" with all the original African backup players and singers. It is wonderful! I recorded that song a few years back. Paul called many years ago, I suppose after he had cut the song in Africa. I had heard the song before, of course, and Paul thought I should record it. I thought it was a wonderful song, but Paul had already done it. He called a few years later and asked me again to consider recording "Graceland." This time I thought I'd better do it.

I was in the middle of recording a CD called *Across the Borderline,* produced by Don Was. When I mentioned "Graceland" to Don, he thought that Paul should produce it. This was a good idea, and I did the best I could, but in my mind I feel that my version wasn't nearly as good as Paul's. This was, and is, his creation, and can only be done by him. This is just my opinion, and of course opinions are like assholes. Everybody has one.

Dᴵᴰ ʏᴏᴜ ʜᴇᴀʀ about the guy in the bar who stood up and said, "All lawyers are assholes!"? Another guy stood up and said, "I take exception to that remark, sir!"

The first guy said, "Are you a lawyer?"

The other guy said, "No, I'm an asshole."

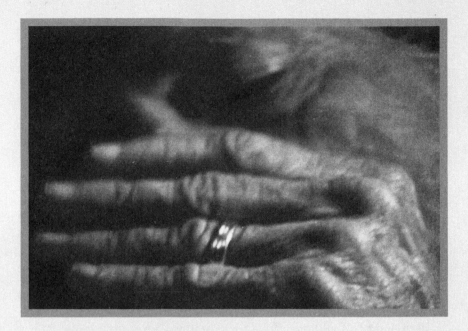

*Ninety-nine percent of the world's lovers are not
with their first choice. That's what makes
the jukebox play.*

Summer of Roses

A short time I have to be with you my love
But a short time is better than no time you see
So I bring to you all my possessions
And would that you'd share them with me

I bring you one springtime of robins
One springtime of robins to sing
And I bring you one summer of roses
One summer of roses I bring

I bring you one autumn of dry leaves
Dry leaves will be helpful you know
To soften the fall of your snowflakes
When I bring you your winter of snow

She's Not for You

Pay no mind to her
She only wants to play
But she's not for you
She's not for you

And I'm the only one
Who would let her act this way
But she's not for you
She's not for you

So she told you she found heaven
In your eyes
Well I think it only fair to warn you
That sometimes she lies

But it's your heart
I can't tell you what to do
But she's not for you
She's not for you

She just looks for greener pastures
Now and then
And when she grows tired she knows Old Faithful
Will just take her back again

So just leave her here
I'm used to feeling blue
She's not for you
She's not for you

You Left Me a Long, Long Time Ago

You tell me today that you're leaving
But just think a while
I'm sure that you must know
Today might be the day that you walk away
But you left me a long, long time ago

Today's just the day that ends it all
  Except the usual memories
  That always linger on
And today might be the day that you walk away
  But you left me a long, long time ago

I stood with helpless hands
And watched me lose your love
  A little more each day
  Then it was gone
And I kept wondering
Just how long until this day would come
Just how long could your pride keep hanging on

So please don't say you're sorry
  Don't say anything
Don't try to say why you must leave
  Just go
And today might be the day that you walk away
  But you left me a long, long time ago

Permanently Lonely

Don't be concerned 'cause it's time I learned
But those who play with fire get burned
But I'll be all right in a little while
But you'll be permanently lonely

And don't be too quick to pity me
Don't salve my heart with sympathy
'Cause I'll be all right in a little while
But you'll be permanently lonely

The world looks on with wonder and pity
    At your kind
'Cause it knows that the future is not very pretty
    For your kind
For your kind will always be running

And wondering what's happened to hearts
That you've broken and left all alone
We'll be all right in a little while
But you'll be permanently lonely

Running lonely

Half a Man

If I only had one arm to hold you
Better yet, if I had none at all
Then I wouldn't have two arms that ached for you
And there'd be one less memory to recall

If I'd only had one ear to listen
To the lies that you told to me
Then I'd more closely resemble
The half a man that you've made of me

If I had been born with but one eye
Then I'd only have one eye that cries
And if half of my heart turned to ashes
Maybe half of my heartaches would die.

If I only had one leg to stand on
Then a much truer picture you'd see
For then I'd more closely resemble
The half a man that you've made of me

So Much To Do

My oatmeal tastes just like confetti
The coffee's too strong so forget it
The toast is burning, so let it
There's just so much to do since you've gone
Too much to do all alone

My tie's lost and I can't find my sweater
There's the doorbell, I hope that's your letter
My head aches, I hope I feel better
There's just so much to do since you've gone
Too much to do all alone

So much to do since you've gone
Too much to do all alone
And time, time rolls on like a river
And oh there's just so much to do
And I just can't do without you

Country Willie

You called me Country Willie
The night you walked away
With the one who promised you a life of joy
You thought my life too simple
And yours was much too gay
To spend it living with a country boy

I'm writing you this letter
I write you every day
I hope that you've received the ones before
But I've heard not one word from you
And every day I pray
That you will not forget your country boy

While you're living in the city
With riches at your door
Is this your love, is this your kind of joy?
Or do you find there's something missing
Does your heart cry out for more?
And do you sometimes miss your country boy?

A cottage in the country
With roses around the door
Could not compete with flashing city lights
But it's all I have to offer
Except for one thing more:
A heart so filled with love that it could die

Well, it's time to end this letter
The light of dawn is near
A lonely night has passed
But there'll be more
Just one more thing in closing
For all the world to hear:
Come home, I love you
      Signed, your country boy

Within Your Crowd

Do you remember
      How they warned you once before?
They made it clear you weren't to see me anymore
Within your world of riches
      Poor boys aren't allowed
So you must learn to love someone
      Within your crowd

Don't you know you're taking chances here with
      me?
You must protect your reputation, don't you see?
Within your social circle I am not allowed
So you must learn to love someone
      Within your crowd

And though I love you more than I can ever say
The danger's much too great and you can't stay

You could never stand dishonor, you're too proud
So you must learn to love someone
    Within your crowd

Someday you'll find someone deserving of your love
Someone to kiss the lips that I'm not worthy of
And when I see you passing by, I'll feel so proud
'Cause though I stand outside, my heart's
    Within your crowd

BUDDY EMMONS AND I WERE in a bar in Nashville. This guy kept bugging us. So Buddy asked the guy, "Are you sure that this is where you want to be?" I gave him half the song.

Are You Sure?

Look around you
Look down the bar from you
The lonely faces that you see
    Are you sure
    That this is where you want to be?

These are your friends
But are they real friends?
And do they love you as much as me?
    Are you sure
    That this is where you want to be?

Please don't let my tears persuade you
I had hoped I wouldn't cry
But lately teardrops seem a part of me

You seem in such a hurry
To lead this kind of life
You've caused so much pain and misery

So look around you and take a good look
And just between you and me
Are you sure
That this is where you want to be?

You Wouldn't Cross the Street (to Say Goodbye)

Today I stood across the street
And watched you leave with him
Right before my disbelieving eyes
And when you saw me standing there
You turned away from me
And you wouldn't even cross the street
To say goodbye

Once you said you'd do most anything
To keep our love
You'd tear out your tongue
Before you'd tell me lies

Once you said you'd go to any lengths
      To be with me
Today you wouldn't even cross the street
      To say goodbye

Once you said you'd crawl on hands and knees
      To be with me
Today you wouldn't even cross the street
      To say goodbye

Bloody Mary Morning

Well it's a bloody mary morning
Baby left me without warning
      Sometime in the night
So I'm flying down to Houston
With forgetting her the nature of my flight

As we taxi toward the runway
With the smog and haze reminding me
      Of how I feel
Just a country boy who's learning
That the pitfalls of the city
      Are extremely real

All the nightlife and parties
Temptation and deceit
      The order of the day

Well it's a bloody mary morning
'Cause I'm leaving baby
  Somewhere in L.A.

Well our golden jet is airborne
And Flight 50 cuts a path
  Across the morning sky
And a voice comes through the speaker
Reassuring us Flight 50
  Is the way to fly
And a hostess takes our order
Coffee, tea, or something stronger
  To start off the day
Well it's a bloody mary morning
'Cause I'm leaving baby
  Somewhere in L.A.

The Sound in Your Mind

Well I've been feeling a little bad
'Cause I've been feeling a little better
  Without you
It's a little like rain
But it's a lot like a sunny day
And it's hard to explain
But the sound of your name
  Don't make music anymore
And it's more like the sound
  Of a love that I lost one day

It's a little too late
To start thinking about starting all over
   I'd rather stay where I am
I can't take another slam
In the mind
I've been feeling a little bad
'Cause I've been feeling a little better
   Without you
But remember my love
   Is the sound that you hear in your mind

I've been running around
Even laughing at half of the memories
And you're not hard to remember
   I just have to think of your name
I've been feeling a little bad
'Cause I've been feeling a little better
   Without you
But remember my love
   Is the sound that you hear in your mind

And remember my love
   Is the sound that you hear in your mind

✴ *It's a quarter to four, April 11.*
  Today fell on a Wednesday.

WE'RE IN HARRISBURG, PENNSYLVANIA. How lucky can you get?
We are headed to sound check pretty soon. Earlier, I got in a nice run

in the rain. One thing about running in the rain, it ain't crowded. Harrisburg has always been a good town for us, and besides, my fan club officers, Dandalion and Daffy, live in the area.

Dandalion has been a fan since the '70s. She never misses a show when we're anywhere in Pennsylvania, and she's done a wonderful job of running our fan club for years. Every night I hear from someone who's a member of the fan club that really enjoys being a member. This is all thanks to you, Daffy and Dandalion. You're the best.

Dandalion is also one of the most well-known DJs in the world. Like Bill Mack, Horace Logan, Ralph Emery, and a few more, they did all they could to keep traditional country music on the airways. I see where Dandalion is being inducted into the Pennsylvania Association of Broadcasters Hall of Fame. Dandy's a DJ on WRK2-FM. She was the first woman to host her own network country music show. She's also an inductee in the National Country Music DJ Hall of Fame. I taped a message to play as she's inducted. It's just a short video to be played on the night of the awards. It said how good she is and how she deserves the award. She has always supported traditional country music and the new country; Garth Brooks, the Dixie Chicks, Alan Jackson, Tim McGraw, Faith Hill, and others.

I never have gotten a lot of radio play through the years, but I knew I was in trouble when I heard someone say, "Boy, I sure wish they would play some of the old guys like Randy Travis and George Strait." But Dandy has always been there for me and all the old farts. God bless you, Dandy. May you have a long and happy life, and congratulations on the award, it couldn't happen to a more deserving person.

Back in Fort Worth in the early '60s, I was just getting started. I had a friend in radio named Bo Powell. He also played all my early records and was a big help in kicking off my career. Thanks, Bo.

———

IT'S STILL RAINING outside as we load up to go to sound check—sister Bobbie, daughter Lana, drivers Gator and L.G., David Anderson, and me. What a crew—bulletproof and invisible all the time. "Bulletproof and invisible" is a Kris Kristofferson phrase. I wonder how he's doing.

I talk to Merle quite a lot. He's still out here, playing, having fun, and drawing great crowds. Merle Haggard is a picking, singing, writing legend. I am probably his biggest fan. We always enjoy playing together and always seem to have entirely too much fun.

Waylon thinks I don't know where he is since he left Nashville, but never fear, ole Willie knows exactly where you are and what you're doing. I have your home under twenty-four-hour surveillance and I've tapped your phone. Just because you live next door to an FBI guy don't mean shit. He's helping me. Just kidding, pal. I hope you're as ornery and mean as you ever were. I want to always remember you that way. I hear from Reggie Young that you're back touring and knocking 'em dead. Keep going.

I received a letter from Johnny Cash inviting me to Jamaica. I think I'm going. Maybe John and I can play some golf. He lives right on a course. John is one of those guys that keeps coming back and coming back. He's got more lives than a cat. It's way too early to be writing him off.

Cash, Waylon, Kris, Haggard, Billy Joe Shaver, me, and a couple more still have a few things to do and say. Amen.

THE GEEZINSLAW BROTHERS are still out there playing, telling jokes, and writing songs. My friend Sam Allred, one half of the Geezinslaw Brothers, is still a DJ and on the air in Austin on KVET. He and Bob

Cole have the #1 show in town. Sam and Son (Dewayne Smith) have performed on all the July 4 Picnics, some of the Farm Aids, and are still drawing crowds wherever they go. Thank God for your help, Sam. All the way back, you were there to help do every crazy and insane thing that I could think of doing.

Sammy talked thousands of people into going out in the middle of fields and pastures all over Texas and sitting in the 100 degree heat, drinking beer, smoking pot with people they wouldn't want to be seen with the day before.

There was something about the mixture of pot, beer, a real hot sun, and a lot of good music that calms the savage beasts somewhere in all of us. We are always afraid of the unknown. It's just natural. But once everyone saw everyone else, heard the music, and baked in the sun all day, I think a healing took place.

We learned that the same spirit lives in all of us. We are the same. There is no difference anywhere in the world. People are people. They laugh, cry, feel, and love, and music seems to be the common denominator that brings us all together. Music cuts through all boundaries and goes right to the soul.

I talked with our editor today. He says he's pleased with the first few pages of this book, and encouraged me to continue on in the same direction. I was telling everyone here how brilliant this person is. There is intelligence out there. There is hope. There is a window. Thank you, Scott, for letting a crazy man loose with a pen, paper, and publisher. "Duh! You've got to roll up the windows!" Amen.

Poodie just came in and told me a joke.

This guy had tennis elbow, and heard about a place that had a urinalysis machine that could analyze your urine and tell you exactly what was wrong with you. Already knowing what he had, he decided to test the machine.

The author at work

The guy poured in a sample of his urine, and the machine coughed and sputtered before spitting out a card that read, YOU HAVE TENNIS ELBOW. The guy was amazed.

He decided to play a trick on the machine. He went home and collected urine specimens from his dog, his daughter, and his wife, and mixed them all together with his own. Feeling smart, he went back to the urinalysis machine and poured in the mixed-up sample.

The machine began to smoke, shake, swell up, and cough. It rattled and clanked before finally spitting out the card that read, YOUR DOG HAS WORMS. YOUR DAUGHTER IS ON CRACK. YOUR WIFE IS CHEATING ON YOU. IF YOU DON'T QUIT JACKING OFF, THAT ELBOW OF YOURS WILL NEVER HEAL.

TIGER WOODS JUST passed Michael Jordan in money from endorsements. Ain't America wonderful or what? Something like a million trillion dollars. I'm not really sure what he's getting, but it's more than I make in a week. Right. Tiger Woods deserves every dollar he gets. He has done a great job of showing young people all over the world the way a superstar should be. He's young, healthy, and so good at golf I can hardly believe it. Good luck, Tiger.

The market made a slight gain this afternoon, then kinda farted and fell back, as Poodie would say. There was a man in Abbott who had all his money tied up in cash. I liked his approach. I think it's more important these days to take care of the principle and forget the interest. But of course a glance at my past brilliant financial choices gives you a clearer picture of just how much I know.

Did I tell you the publisher liked the book? These are amazingly intelligent people. No wonder they are where they are.

———

THERE WAS A GUY IN A HOUSE of ill repute making love to a girl in a room, on a bed next to an open window. They worked their way over too close to the window and fell out. They hit the ground and never missed a beat. They just kept working. A drunk came by and saw the couple screwing in the street in front of the whorehouse. The drunk walked up to the front door and knocked. A lady came to the door and the drunk said, "Madam, your sign fell down."

KINKY WANTED ME TO TELL YOU THIS JOKE. . . .

A lady reporter went into an insane asylum to do an exposé on the treatment of patients. She had heard there were some very interesting things going on and wanted to get to the bottom of it. Once inside the asylum, she met a patient who offered to help her get her story. He was a computer expert and turned out to be very helpful in securing information that the reporter could use.

When she had gathered all the information that she needed, she said to the guy helping her, "Sir, you are so smart. You have been so very helpful. I couldn't have gotten all this information without you. Tell me, how did you wind up here?"

He said, "Lady, I'm just as sane as anybody. I don't know. I woke up one day and I was here."

She said, "Thanks so much for your help and information. When I leave here, I'm going to do everything in my power to get you out."

As she walked to the door the guy picked up a Coke bottle and threw it at her, hitting her right behind the ear. He yelled, "Don't forget!"

Phases and stages
Circles and cycles
Scenes that we've all seen before
Let me tell you some more

Washing the Dishes

Washing the dishes
Scrubbing the floors
> *Caring for someone*
> *Who don't care anymore*
Learning to hate all the things
That she once loved to do
> *Like washing his shirts*
> *And never complaining*
Except of red stains on the collars
> *Ironing and crying*
> *Crying and ironing*
Caring for someone who don't care anymore
Someday she'll just walk away

Walkin'

After carefully considering
> *The whole situation*
I stand with my back to the wall

Walkin' is better
      Than running away
And crawling ain't no good at all

And if guilt is the question
      Then truth is the answer
And I've been lying to me all along
There ain't nothing worth saving
      Except one another
And before you wake up I'll be gone

'Cause after carefully considering
      The whole situation
I stand with my back to the wall
Walkin' is better
      Than running away
And crawling ain't no good at all

Sister's Coming Home

Sister's coming home
Mama's gonna let her sleep
      The whole day long
      The whole day long
Sister's coming home
Mama's gonna let her sleep the whole day long

Sister's coming home
Mama don't like the man
> *That done her wrong, Lord, that done her*
> > *wrong*
Sister's coming home
Mama don't like the man that done her wrong

Sister's coming home
Mama's gonna let her sleep
> *The whole day long*
> *The whole day long*
Sister's coming home
Mama's gonna let her sleep the whole day long
And her mirror's gonna tell her how long she's
> *been gone*

Down at the Corner Beer Joint

Down at the corner beer joint
Dancing to the rock 'n' roll
> *Sister likes to do it, Lord*
> *Sister likes to move her soul*

Down at the corner beer joint
Dancing on the hardwood floor
> *Her jeans fit a little bit tighter*
> *Than they did before*

Than they did before
Than they did before
Lord her jeans fit a little bit tighter
Than they did before
Than they did before
Than they did before
Oh her jeans fit a little bit tighter
   Than they did before

I'm Falling in Love Again

I'm falling in love again
I never thought I would again
   I never thought I could

And I may be making mistakes again
But if I lose or win
   How will I know?

How will I know?
How will I know?
How will I know?

And I'm falling in love again
If I lose or win
   How will I know?

✳ 4:05 *P.M.*, *Sewell, New Jersey*

HEADED TO SOUND CHECK, listening to last night's show. Sounds pretty tight. I hope we can do as well tonight.

Lana's beans are delicious. She makes life on the bus a lot more fun. She and sister Bobbie are always asking me if I need food, clothes, shampoo, or whatever. They spoil me rotten. It doesn't affect me. I'm still the same old guy I always was—spoiled rotten.

✳ 6:50 *P.M.*, *Sewell, New Jersey*

SOUND CHECK IS OVER. We are parked across the street from McQuedy Something or Other. If you enjoy the look of prisons, you'll dig this place. Then I see Jackie and Paul and a lot of people coming out of a side door. It looks like a prison break. Very scary.

I was listening to "The Great Divide," and by the way, have I told you that the publisher likes the book?

We are doing some music from the *Rainbow Connection* CD in the shows. The band and I are still working on the "Rainbow Connection" song itself. I think it's about ready. Paul Williams, the writer of "Rainbow Connection," and I are both being inducted into the Songwriters Hall of Fame this year, in June, I think. Now there's a co-inky-dinky for you.

Fortunately, we're not in control.

While filming a Disney movie, *The Country Bears,* last month in Los Angeles, I played some of the *Rainbow Connection* CD to the producers, and they may use some of the music in the movie. Talk about coincidence, the Jim Henson Company (Jim was the voice of Kermit the Frog and first sang "Rainbow Connection" in *The Muppet Movie*) was doing the special-effects work in the Disney movie, so I played them the song too. Thank you, Walt. Thank you, Jim.

DID YOU HEAR ABOUT THE DRUNK who was walking down the street when a guy carrying a huge grandfather clock came out of an antique store and bumped into him? The drunk accidentally knocked the antique collector into the clock, breaking it into a thousand pieces. The man with the clock said, "Why don't you watch where you're going?"

The drunk looked at the guy and said, "Why don't you carry a wristwatch like everybody else?"

✳ *1:15 A.M., Good Friday the 13th*

ON THE WAY TO Union County Arts Center in Rahway, New Jersey. Tonight's crowd in Sewell was fantastic. A lot of fans both young and old waited a long time after the show while I signed autographs. At the end of the line, as they always are, never getting in front of anyone even though they know they could at any time, were two of my favorite fans. Katie and Jill must be at least fourteen years old by now. They've been coming to the shows for more than half their lives. I feel like they are mine. They never miss a show when we are within a four- or five-hundred-mile radius. Girls, I hope you always come see us, we'd miss you a lot if you didn't. They're twins—I can never tell them apart, except that Katie always walks up first, so I know the other one is Jill. I'm so smart, sometimes I amaze me. Right.

———

HAVE I TOLD YOU that the publisher likes the book?

A LADY HAD BEEN grocery shopping. Walking to her car, she tripped and broke her paper bag of groceries, containing a gallon of water, a dozen eggs, and a pound of bacon. Everything splattered all over the pavement. The lady was so upset, she started crying. A drunk walked up, surveyed the situation, and said, "Don't cry, lady. It wouldn't have lived anyway. Its eyes are too far apart."

So You Think You're a Cowboy

So you think you're a cowboy
But you're only a kid
With a mind to do everything wrong
And it starts to get smoother
When the circle begins
But by the time that you get there, it's gone

So you think you're a winner
But you're losing again
The cards have already been dealt
And the hand that you're playing
Means nothin' at all
And knowing is all that is left

So live life as you find it
The best that you can
Tomorrow cannot right the wrong
Don't wait for tomorrow
To bring you your dreams
'Cause by the time that you get there, they're gone

FYI: JOHN WAYNE COULDN'T SING, AND HIS HORSE WAS NOT VERY SMART

After the show tonight, some sweet lady, Diane is her name, gave me two Gene Autry and Roy Rogers guitars. She said that she also has a Hopalong Cassidy guitar that she'll give me. I'm proud of them since these were, are, and always will be, three of my heroes.

Another one of the educational advantages of living in Abbott and Hill County was that you got to see Roy, Hoppy, and Gene every Saturday at the Ritz Theater in Hillsboro, ten miles north of Abbott. For twenty cents you could ride on the train, the interurban, from Abbott to Hillsboro and back. The movie cost six cents. Once again, Roy, Gene, and Hoppy have shown us how to be the best cowboys.

Back then, everything was real simple. The good guys wore white hats and the bad guys wore black hats, and the good cowboys always won. What the heck happened? Now the bad guys win all the time. Of course, it's hard to tell the bad guys from the good guys.

If I had my way, Gene, Roy, and Hoppy movies would be required viewing in every school in the world. And if I'm elected, this will come to pass. Of course, I ain't running for anything.

Where Do You Stand?

From somewhere behind you
You've come with your suitcase in hand
Hey, what's your plan?
  Where do you stand?

The world's still divided
And you're still undecided
Decide if you can
Hey, what's your plan
  Where do you stand?

Where do you stand?
Where do you stand?
Hey, what's your plan?
Where do you stand?

It's time for commitment
It's time for a showing of hands
Hey, what's your plan?
  Where do you stand?

Surely there's someone
  With courage
To say where he stands
Hey, what's your plan?
  Where do you stand?

"Where Do You Stand" is a half-assed political song that I wrote several years ago. Back when there was talk, and some truth, that I was thinking about running for a senate office in Texas. I'm glad I didn't. My liver couldn't have taken all the cocktail parties. I wound up giving the song to the Ralph Yarborough campaign. He was more suited for that line of work.

We have just pulled into somewhere. Maybe a truck stop. Maybe the motel. This is exciting. I can't wait to see which one it is. If it's a truck stop, I'll stay on the bus. If it's a motel, I'll stay on the bus. Don't get me wrong. I don't mind. I was just being factitious, I think. I'll look that up. If *factitious* doesn't apply, I'll have another big word in there before a cat can lick its ass. We authors deal in words. You can't tell a songwriter he ain't any good because he knows better.

Did I tell you the publishers like the book? You don't pile up that kind of wisdom in schools, Bubba. Some people are just born wise.

Of course, I believe in reincarnation. I believe you keep coming back until you get wise. Then if you want to come back again to show off a little, that's OK too. It's all right to come back a few times just to be wise, just so other people can see you and say, "Damn, he's wise."

Changing Skies

> *There's a bird in the sky*
> > *Flying high, flying high*
> *To a place from a place*
> > *Changing skies, changing skies*

> *There are clouds in the sky*
> *Clouds of fear and despair*

Love like ours never dies
     Changing skies, changing skies

Little bird have you heard
Freedom lies, freedom lies
But love like ours never dies
     Just changing skies, changing skies

Tougher Than Leather

He was tougher than leather
And he didn't care whether
     The sun shined or not
When a young kid from Cowtown
Wanted a showdown
He was careless or maybe forgot

But he died in a gunfight
Blinded by sunlight
     Never draw when you're facing the sun
And old Tougher Than Leather
Just carved one more notch on his gun

And when he turned to go
The beautiful maiden knelt down
     Where her dead sweetheart lay
And on his breast placed a rose
While the townspeople stared in dismay

And old Tougher Than Leather
Should've known better
    But he picked up the rose in his hand
And the townspeople froze
When his hands crushed the rose
And the rose petals fell in the sand

And old Tougher Than Leather
Was a full-time go-getter
    The grass never grew beneath his feet
From one town to another
He would ride like the wind
But his mind kept going back to the street

Where a young cowboy died
And a young maiden cried
    And rose petals fell in the sand
And his heart had been softened
By the beautiful maiden
And he knew he must see her again

Well he went back to the town
Where it all had come down
    And he searched but his search was in vain
He had wanted to find her
And say he was sorry
For causing her heart so much pain

But one night he died
From a poison inside
    Brought on by the wrong he had done

And old Tougher Than Leather
Had carved his last notch on his gun

He was buried in Cowtown
Along about sundown
    Looking good in his new store-bought
      clothes
When the young maiden came over
And knelt down beside him
And on his lapel placed a rose

Somewhere in Texas (Part I)

Somewhere in Texas
    A young cowboy dreams
Of the days when the buffalo roamed
And he wished he had lived then
    'Cause he knew he could have been
The best cowboy the world had ever known

He went dancing that night
    With his San Antone rose
The one he would marry someday
To the music of Bob Wills
    And polkas and waltzes
While beautiful time passed away

Somewhere in Texas (Part II)

Going home in his pickup
      Not knowing a stickup
Was in progress on the same side of town
By a man in a truck
      The same kind he was driving
Bad karma was soon coming down

Before the store owner died
      He had tried to describe
The man who had shot him that day
And he described to the letter
      The innocent cowboy
So they tried him and sent him away

My Love for the Rose

Was it something I did, Lord
      A lifetime ago?
Am I just now repaying a debt that I owe?

Justice, sweet justice
      You travel so slow
But you can't change my love for the rose

Little Old-Fashioned Karma

It's just a little old-fashioned karma coming down
Just a little old-fashioned justice going round
     A little bit of sowing
     And a little bit of reaping
     A little bit of laughing
     And a little bit of weeping
Just a little old-fashioned karma coming down

Coming down
Coming down
Just a little old-fashioned karma
     Coming down
It really ain't hard to understand
If you're gonna dance
     You gotta pay the band
It's just a little old-fashioned karma coming down

Nobody Slides, My Friend

Nobody slides, my friend
It's a truth on which you can depend
If you're living a lie
It will eat you alive
Nobody slides, my friend

Nobody slides, my friend
You can try it but you'll never win
You can scream, you can shout
But it all evens out
And nobody slides, my friend

Nobody slides, my friend
Listen I'll say it again
You can run, you can hide
But it's still waiting inside
And nobody slides, my friend

I Am the Forest

I'll always be with you
For as long as you please
  For I am the forest
  But you are the trees

I'm empty without you
So come grow within me
  For I am the forest
  And you are the trees

And the heavens need romance
So love never dies
  So you be the stars, dear
  And I'll be the sky

And should enemies find us
Let them all be forewarned
  That you are the thunder
  And I am the storm

And I'll always be with you
For as long as you please
  For I am the forest
  And you are the trees

I'll always be with you
For as long as you please
  For I am the forest
  But you are the trees

Well, we are here, at the motel. I may be back, but in case I'm not, re-member Elvis's last words, "Corn? I don't remember corn."

Jackie King wanted me to tell you this one. This guy is playing piano in a bar. He said, "You are about the sorriest bunch of creepy-looking assholes I have ever had to perform in front of. Now here's a little toe-tapper for you. . . ."

ALSO THERE'S THE one about the girl who came to a club one night. She was talking to the guitar player in the band and said, "I just want you to know that I watched you play tonight. There was something very spe-cial about the way that your fingers just flew up and down the neck of your guitar. It turned me on so much, there were times when I wanted to grab you and screw your brains out!"

The guitar player said, "Did you catch the first show or the second?"

For extra protection, please cover your organ before sex, or at least throw a sheet over the piano.

"Perfect pitch": When you toss an accordion into the trash can and it hits a banjo. Just kidding. I love the banjo and the accordion. My friend Paul Buskirk wrote a song called, "You Just Can't Play a Sad Song on the Banjo," and Flaco Jimenez brought new dimensions to the accordion. These guys and many other great musicians have always proven there are no bad instruments, but there are a few bad pickers. And then again, maybe you shouldn't play a sad song on the banjo.

The most horrifying sound in the world has got to be a beginner violinist. It sounds like chalk on a blackboard. I tried playing fiddle a few times. I just couldn't stand hearing me. How do people ever stay with it long enough to get past the bad notes?

However, I don't believe players like Stephane Grappelli and Johnny Gimble ever hit a bad note in their life. If they ever did, they turned it into a hot lick so fast nobody caught it.

Speaking of Stephane Grappelli, I must mention the greatest guitar player who ever lived, Django Reinhardt. Stephane and Django played together many years ago. This is undeniably the best music I have ever heard.

———

A YOUNG KID JOINED THE ARMY. He wanted to be a hero. He volunteered to go overseas to the front lines. It was 1944 and we were at war with Japan. The young soldier went to his sergeant and announced he wanted to be a hero. The sergeant said, "Oh you do? Well, here's what you do, son. Just walk over there about a half mile and yell, 'Hirohito is a son of a bitch!' The enemy will show itself and you just shoot one and bring him back and you'll be a hero."

So the young soldier walked off toward the road where the enemy lay waiting. After about an hour he came back bleeding, bruised, and half dead. The sergeant asked what happened. The soldier said, "I did just what you said. I went there and stood up and yelled, 'Hirohito is a son of a bitch!' A Japanese soldier stood up and said, 'Harry Truman is a son of a bitch!' We were standing in the middle of the road shaking hands when a truck hit us."

✳ *3:09 A.M., Good Friday the 13th*

REMEMBER, THE EARLY BIRD GETS THE WORM, but the second mouse gets the cheese. 'Nite all . . .

✳ *11:50 A.M.*

LEONARD NIMOY IS NARRATING A STORY, *The History of Christianity*. This part is all about John the Baptist. We are at a Holiday Inn across from a CVC pharmacy and food mart with a one-hour photo service. I must be the luckiest guy in the world: at a Holiday Inn where there are never any surprises, and a drugstore right across the street. God is good.

Rahway, New Jersey, looks a lot like Sewell, New Jersey. I went for a short run this morning. Actually, very short. I couldn't get into it. No energy today. Some days are like that. Maybe it's a day of rest. My Sabbath. Maybe I won't do a sound check today.

There must be a better way to start the day than getting up. I could sleep my life away, I believe, if I let myself. Maybe I won't do anything except the show tonight. Maybe I'll just nap all day. What's wrong with that? Sleep is an escape on a lazy day. Just because you take a day off don't mean you're lazy. Well, what's wrong with being lazy sometimes?

> *Well, I might have gone fishing,*
> *Got to thinking it over*
> *The road to the river is a mighty long way*
> *It must be the season, no rhyme or no reason*
> *Taking it easy. It's my lazy day*

Thank you, Smiley Burnette.

REMEMBER THE MA-AND-PA JOKES? Ma said, "Pa, your foot is in the fire."

Pa said, "Which one, Ma?"

That's me today. I just sit around and think deep thoughts, like, How deep is a hole? What are the differences in dust particles? There must be some or else why are there so many of them? One dust particle really would have been plenty.

Oh, I just remembered. It's almost April 15! Don't forget to file your toenails by midnight!

Yesterday's Wine

Miracles appear in the strangest of places
Fancy meeting you here
The last time I saw you was just out of Houston
Sit down, let me buy you a beer

Your presence is welcome
With me and my friend here
This is a hangout of mine
We come here quite often and listen to music
Partaking of yesterday's wine

Yesterday's wine
Yesterday's wine
Aging with time
Like yesterday's wine
Yesterday's wine
Yesterday's wine
We're aging with time
Like yesterday's wine

You give the appearance of one widely traveled
I'll bet you've seen things in your time
So sit down beside me and tell me your story
If you think you'll like yesterday's wine

Yesterday's wine
Yesterday's wine
> *Aging with time*
> *Like yesterday's wine*
Yesterday's wine
Yesterday's wine
>> *We're aging with time*
>> *Like yesterday's wine*

✳ Monday, April 16, 7 P.M.

JUST FINISHED MY SECOND RUN for today. I'm trying to get ready for a run in Austin on October 21, a benefit for Farm Aid. The run is sponsored by the city of Austin, *Runner's World,* New Balance, RunTex, and hopefully twenty thousand runners.

A press conference was held in Boston at the Hard Rock Cafe to promote the run in Austin. Everyone was already in town for the Boston Marathon, which was today. The winning time for the men was two hours and nine minutes, and the winning time for the women was two hours and fourteen minutes. A lot of people from Farm Aid, New Balance, and *Runner's World* were there. It turned out to be a very positive press conference. We all agreed to make the run in Austin a huge success for Farm Aid, and I'm sure it will be.

David was reminding me of our first Farm Aid concert. Thanks to our old friend Buddy Lee, we were able to pull it off. With only twenty-one days to go, Buddy gave us a hundred thousand dollars to promote it. We made more money on that first concert than we have since. Buddy, you were a great friend and a credit to your profession, or all your many professions.

Buddy was a professional wrestler turned talent promoter, and opened a booking agency in Nashville, the Buddy Lee Talent Agency, of which I was proud to be with. We had many happy years and times together. Thank you, Buddy Lee, wherever you are.

Also we can't forget our friend Paul Corbin and The Nashville Network for coming to the rescue. They offered to broadcast three hours of the first Farm Aid. I said at a press conference they would broadcast all twelve hours, and they did. I think they were glad they did—I know I was. I hear that Paul's at BMI now, replacing Roger Sovine. I know he'll do a good job there. Thanks, Paul.

TODAY IS TAX DAY, and it's all over the TV. I think you should be able to write a letter to your tax man explaining to him how your tax bill is way too high and there must be some way to work it out. The letters would then be rated on originality and sincerity. The winner would never have to pay their taxes again. Kinda like a contest. The first million winners would live tax-free forever. The rest of the letter writers would be awarded a deferment on their taxes. What do you think?

THERE'S A GUY on TV lifting eleven pounds of iron with his eyelids. That reminds me of the guy who went to a house of ill repute. When the madam opened the door, the man said, "I would like to experience something different. Do you have anything on your menu that would be different than anything I've ever experienced? I'll be happy to pay you well."

The madam said, "Sir, you're in luck! I know just the girl for you. Her name is Alice, in room 601."

The guy goes to room 601 and opens the door. Alice comes to the door. The guy explains how he wants something different, and Alice says, "Have you ever been winked off?"

"No, I don't think I have. What is that?"

"I'll show you." Alice reached up and pulled out her glass eye. She said, "Just put it in."

He did, and they did, and when it was all over he said, "My God. That was the best sex I've ever had. When I'm back in town, I want to come back here to see you."

She said, "Great! I'll keep an eye out for you."

L.G. AND DAVID have gone to Denny's, and Gator is probably sleeping. This is a day off and I'm alone on the bus. Lana went home for some physical therapy on her neck. I know she'll be fine in a little while. So, sister Bobbie fed me breakfast this morning—bacon, ham and eggs. A fan gave me the ham last night at the show. I've been eating on it all day.

When I recorded the *Red Headed Stranger* album, I had in mind doing a *Red Headed Stranger* movie to go along with it. I had a big dream of an album and movie out at the same time, each promoting the other. It didn't work out that way. It was ten years after the album came out before I could make the movie. My idea of having them come out together was down the drain already by then. However, I still thought the movie was a good idea.

I went to my friend Bill Wittliff who had written the movie *Barbarosa,* and asked him to write the *RHS* script, and he did. He wrote a great script but we still needed the money. I asked my friend Don Tyson for some seed money. He came through, along with a few other close friends. A banker in Austin agreed to handle the *RHS* movie account. An Austin investment company had agreed to come up with the rest of the movie money, and we were in business.

The Red Headed Stranger

There were disagreements between me and the investment company, so they dropped out, leaving us in the middle of the first week of shooting. You have a hundred-thousand-dollar-a-week payroll to meet, and your backer backs out. Well, I started writing hot checks. The banker, for whatever reason, never bounced a single check. I guess he liked me and believed I would eventually pay up.

I had done an interview with Cheryl McCall and *People* magazine. She was now covering the making of *RHS* for *Life* magazine. She knew all about the money guys falling out and the banker staying with me. She went back to the East Coast and was telling our story to Carolyn Mugar, who we later nicknamed the "Mysterious Woman from Boston." Carolyn turned out to be a huge fan of mine and asked Cheryl how much did I need to make the movie? To make a long story short, she brought down a check large enough to cover my hot checks and enough to finish the whole movie. Needless to say, she is still one of my closest friends, and now runs our Farm Aid offices in Cambridge, Massachusetts. Thank you, God, for Carolyn Mugar.

Time of the Preacher

> *It was the time of the preacher*
> *When the story began*
> *The choice of a lady*
> *And a love of a man*
> *And how he loved her so dearly*
> *He went out of his mind*
> *When she left him for someone*
> *She'd left behind*

He cried like a baby
He screamed like a panther
       In the middle of the night
And he saddled his pony
And went for a ride
It was the time of the preacher
In the year of '01
       Now the preaching is over
       And the lesson's begun

Blue Rock Montana

Well, he rode into Blue Rock
Dusty and tired
And he got him a room for the night
And he lay there in silence
With too much on his mind
Still hoping that he was not right

But he found them that evening
At a tavern in town
In a quiet little out-of-the-way place
And they smiled at each other
When he walked through the door
And they died with their smiles on their faces
They died with a smile on their face

The Red Headed Stranger

The red headed stranger from Blue Rock Montana
Rode into town one day
And under his knees was a raging black stallion
And walking behind was a bay
The red headed stranger had eyes like the thunder
His lips they were sad and tight
For his little lost love lay asleep on the hillside
And his heart was heavy as night

Don't cross him
Don't boss him
He's wild in his sorrow
He's riding and hiding his pain
Don't fight him, don't spite him, just wait
till tomorrow
And maybe he'll ride on again

A yellow haired woman leaned out of her window
Watched as he passed her way
She drew back in fear at the sight of the stallion
But cast greedy eyes on the bay
He bought her a drink and he gave her some
money
He just didn't seem to care
She followed him out as he saddled his stallion
Laughed as she grabbed at the bay

He shot her so quick they had no time to warn her
She never heard anyone say

Don't cross him
Don't boss him
He's wild in his sorrow
He's riding and hiding his pain
Don't fight him, don't spite him, just wait
      till tomorrow
And maybe he'll ride on again

The yellow haired woman was buried at sunset
The stranger went free of course
You can't hang a man for killing a woman
That's trying to steal your horse
Now this is the tale of the red headed stranger
And if he should pass your way
Stay out of the path of the raging black stallion
And don't lay a hand on the bay

Don't cross him
Don't boss him
He's wild in his sorrow
He's riding and hiding his pain
Don't fight him, don't spite him, just wait
      till tomorrow
And maybe he'll ride on again

Denver

The bright lights of Denver
Are shining like diamonds
        Like ten thousand jewels in the sky
And it's nobody's business where you're going
Or where you come from
And you're judged by the look in your eye

She saw him that evening
In a tavern in the town
In a quiet little out-of-the-way place
And they smiled at each other
As he walked through the doors
And they danced with their smiles on their faces
And they danced with a smile on their faces

I Guess I've Come to Live Here in Your Eyes

I guess I've come to live here in your eyes
This must be the place called paradise
        You are so precious to me
And what a special time within our lives
So I guess I've come to live here in your eyes

A thousand times I see you
And a thousand times you take my breath away

On the bus, early morning

And fears and doubts consume me
I'm afraid someone will take it all away

I hope I'm here forever
But I think it's time that we both realized
That I guess I've come to live here in your eyes

I am still on the bus between a Holiday Inn and a cornfield. We're just outside Somewhere, Pennsylvania, watching the Mississippi flooding on CNN. It makes these Pennsylvania cornfields look very nice.

Did you hear about the drunk who leaned a little too close to a two-story apartment building window and fell out? He was laying on the sidewalk when someone ran up and asked what happened. The drunk looked up and said, "Hell I don't know. I just got here."

THE NEW *RAINBOW CONNECTION* CDs just arrived so I can give some out to the press. Island Records once again came through like a champ. The David Zettner art work is exceptional, and I'm happy to see a photo of me and Dean Bird, my great-grandson. He's the son of my beautiful granddaughter Martha and Matt Hubbard, who's a musician and engineer, and the coproducer of *Rainbow Connection*. Matt Hubbard, remember that name. I believe you'll be hearing a lot more from him in the future.

❊ *6:10 P.M., Easter, Pennsylvania*

THE STATE THEATER IS ON MY RIGHT and Church Street on my left. Did I tell you the publishers liked the book? Some of the best jokes I hear I get from the kids, *my* kids of course. Since Paula is a blonde, I get all the blonde jokes.

I like the one about the blonde twins. One was on one side of the room, and one was on the other. One blonde said, "Come over here" to her twin, who replied, "Hell, I am already over there!"

✳ *7:00 P.M.*

LOU DOUGHERTY CAME BY THE BUS just a few moments ago. Lou is one of the oldest fans I have, and she's not really that old, we're about the same age. There is not a better fan in the world and I'm always glad to see her. She has probably seen over a hundred of our shows. If we're anywhere in Pennsylvania, she will be there. I forgot to ask her why she wasn't in Hershey the other night. She wasn't in Williamsport either. She has a lot of explaining to do.

It's a cold and rainy night. Some places in Pennsylvania are expecting snow. It was 85 degrees and sunny in Austin. It's OK though; I could be by the Mississippi River which is on the way to its highest crest ever. One guy on TV was pouring water out of his house. He said, "Well, when you live by a river, things will happen."

I admire his courage and tenacity. But I'd still rather be on Church Street parked behind the State Theater, safe and dry on our Honeysuckle Rose #3. Honeysuckle #1 we wore out. Honeysuckle #2 we wrecked in Nova Scotia. We have over a half a million miles on #3.

THERE WAS JUST SOME LADY on CNN holding a sign that was very negative about drinking milk. I have heard all this bullshit about how bad dairy products are. I would like to say on behalf of dairy products that I have eaten eggs, bacon, and butter, and I drank plenty of milk my whole life. I am sixty-eight years old and in damn good shape. I do exercise quite a bit, and now I have started drinking skim milk. I have been on a no-sugar diet now for a few days. No fries, no bread, nothing with sugar. Nothing that will turn to sugar once eaten. Eggs, eggs, and more eggs. Now I would like to ask the lady holding the "no milk" sign just what is your problem? Why do you care whether or not I drink milk? As long as I drink milk responsibly, why is it any of your business? Get a life, lady. Eat more ice cream and lighten up, you'll live a longer life, or at least you won't be pissing people off by trying to run theirs.

I grew up in Abbott on the edge of town. We had a milk cow, chickens, and a garden. I raised a fat calf and a fat hog every year. I was a Future Farmer of America and proud to be one. The fresh organic vegetables from our garden and the livestock could not have been healthier. Now, I admit, nowadays when you buy eggs, meat, and milk, it's not the same. There's additives to give the milk a longer shelf life, and growth hormones given to the chickens and the cattle. Nothing tastes the same these days. Eggs coming from hens walking around on just a little bit of concrete eating questionable foods as opposed to eggs coming from chickens allowed to roam around scratching for worms, there is no comparing the taste.

Will You Remember Mine?

Sweet is the song when the song is love
Love that has stood the test of time
And when you've heard all the songs of love
Will you remember mine?

Gone are the times when I held you close
And pressed your lips to mine
Now when you kiss another's lips
        Will you remember mine?

I have sat beneath the trees
While the cool summer breeze
        Blew away the sands of time
And thought of days when you were near
Remembering when you were mine

Gone are the times when I walked with you
And held your hand in mine
Now when you hold another's hand
        Will you remember mine?

✻ *Wednesday, April 19, Lowell, Massachusetts,*
   3:20 P.M.

WOKE UP THIS MORNING and looked out the bus window and saw snow, so I decided to go for a run. I started running and realized I was running around a golf course. Just my luck. The motel is next to a nine-hole golf course and it's snowing. I don't believe it.

This looks like a December day
This looks like a time-to-remember day
And I remember a spring
        Such a sweet tender thing

Where love's summer college,
And the green leaves of knowledge
Were waiting to fall with the Fall
And where September wine
    Numbed a measure of time
    Through the tears of October
    Now November's over
And this looks like a December day

This looks like a December day
It looks like we've come to the end of the way
And as my memories race back to
    Love's eager beginning
Reluctant to play with the thoughts of the ending
The ending that won't go away
And as my memories race back to
Love's eager beginning
Reluctant to play with the thoughts of the ending
    The ending that won't go away
And this looks like a December day

✳ *11:55 P.M., same day*

THIS LADY WAS LAYING ON THE FLOOR without any clothes on doing her Jane Fonda workout. Her husband came in just as she was on her back with her legs up in the air. He said, "Honey, get up and put in your teeth and comb your hair. You're looking more and more like your mother every day!"

✷ *12:35 A.M., next day, same night*

WE'RE ON THE WAY TO Trenton, New Jersey, and the War Memorial Auditorium, coming from the Lowell, Massachusetts Memorial Auditorium tonight, our last night. I know, I'm confused myself.

I used to play the White Horse bowling alley in Trenton several years ago. I'll bet it's not even there now. After Trenton we'll head to New York City and the Beacon Theater. I'm doing an interview with Dan Rather. That should be fun. He's an old Texas buddy. The other night he was the speaker and a presenter for the first Texas Artist Achievement Award, which I proudly received. He's a good man and I'm proud to know him.

I love playing in New York City. I love walking down the streets and running in Central Park. I remember going to see Kris and Rita at Radio City Music Hall one time. On the way back home I wrote . . .

> *We were headed home in Austin*
> *Caught pneumonia on the road*
> > *Taking it home to Connie and the kids*
> *A wheel ran off and jumped a railroad*
> *Then ran through a grocery store*
> > *If you want to buy a bus I'm taking bids*
>
> *Well I just got back from New York City*
> *Kris and Rita done it all*
> > *Raw perfection there for all the world to see*
> *Lord I heard an angel singing*

In the Philharmonic Hall
> *Rita Coolidge, Rita Coolidge cleft for me*

And the devil shivered in his sleeping bag
He said traveling on the road is a fucking drag
If we can make it home by Friday we can brag
And the devil shivered in his sleeping bag

I did an album in New York City one time. It turned out to be called *Shotgun Willie.* I wrote the title song while I was making the album. Jerry Wexler was the producer—one of the best producers of all time. I had met him at Harlan Howard's Christmas party. I was looking for a record deal and he really liked my work. So there we were in New York City, doing an album. I was thrilled. At the same time though I was a little pissed because I wanted to come up with a really good new song for the album.

Shotgun Willie

Shotgun Willie
> *Sits around in his underwear*
Biting on a bullet
> *And pulling out all of his hair*
Shotgun Willie's
> *Got all of his family there*

(I pretty much did too. Sister Bobbie, me, Jimmy Day, Larry Gatlin, Jerry Wexler.)

Well you can't make a record
    If you ain't got nothing to say
Well you can't make a record
    If you ain't got nothing to say
You can't play music
    If you don't know nothing to play

Now John T. Flores
    Was working for the Ku Klux Klan
At six-foot-five
    John T. was a helluva man
Made a lot of money
    Selling sheets on the family plan

Shotgun Willie
    Sits around in his underwear
Biting on a bullet
    And pulling out all of his hair
Shotgun Willie's
    Got all of his family there

It's the only song I ever wrote in New York City. Maybe I'll write another one this time.

Every song is a gospel song. All music is sacred. Every note of music in the universe is spiritual and sacred . . . and that's the gospel truth. Amen

Our Father who art in Heaven
Hallowed be Thy name

Thy kingdom come, Thy will be done
On earth as it is in heaven
Give us this day our daily bread
And forgive us our sins
As we forgive those who sin against us
Lead us not into temptation and deliver us
        from evil
For Thine is the kingdom, the power, and
        the glory forever
Amen

This is an affirmation that you can always repeat, whether you're going to bed or headed into a fist fight. It always seems to help me. I keep it on a loop in my mind. It's programmed to kick in whenever I keep my mind open and my mouth shut. Feel free to use it if you want to. I didn't write it, but I highly recommend it.

I Thought About You

I thought about trees
And how much I'd like to climb one
I thought about friends
And how rare it is to find one
I thought about You
The most dearest, sweet and kind one
I thought about You, Lord
I thought about You

I thought about life
And the way that things are going
I thought about love
And the pain there is in growing
I thought about You
The One who is all knowing
I thought about You, Lord
I thought about You

I thought about You
And the songs that I've been singing
I thought about You
And the joy that they keep bringing
I thought about You
A love that's never ending
I thought about You, Lord
I thought about you

In God's Eyes

Never think evil thoughts of anyone
It's just as wrong to think as to say
For a thought is but a word that's unspoken
    In God's eyes
    He sees it this way

Lend a hand if you can to a stranger
Never worry if he can't repay

For in time you'll be repaid ten times over
        In God's eyes
        He sees it this way

In God's eyes we're like sheep in a meadow
Now and then a lamb goes astray
And open arms should await its returning
        In God's eyes
        He sees it this way

It's Not for Me to Understand

I passed a home the other day
The yard was filled with kids at play
And on the sidewalk of this home
A little boy stood all alone

His smiling face was sweet and kind
But I could see the boy was blind
He listened to the children play
I bowed my head and there I prayed

Dear Lord above, why must this be?
And then these words came down to me
After all you're just a man
And it's not for you to understand

It's not for you to reason why
You too are blind without my eyes

So question not what I command
'Cause it's not for you to understand

Now when I pray my prayer is one
I pray His will, not mine, be done
After all I'm just a man
And it's not for me to understand

Laying My Burdens Down

Well I used to walk stooped
 From the weight of my tears
 But I just started laying my burdens down
I used to duck bullets from the rifle of fear
 I just started laying my burdens down

Oh I'm layin' 'em down
I just started laying my burdens down
Oh I'm layin' 'em down
I just started laying my burdens down

The flesh ain't nothing but the bark on a tree
 I just started laying my burdens down
The tree ain't nothing but the soul in me
 I just started laying my burdens down

Soul took love on a helluva ride
 I just started laying my burdens down

Soul ain't nothing but the car love drives
I just started laying my burdens down

Love said, "Mama, can I come on home?"
I just started laying my burdens down
And God said, "Son you ain't never been gone"
I just started laying my burdens down

"Physician, heal thyself," and "Do unto others as you would have them do unto you," are my two favorite lines from the Bible. Here's another great prayer: "Let nothing but good come to me. Let nothing but good go from me."

JUST OPENED MY little red New Testament and it says in Proverbs, chapter 6, verse 4: "Give not sleep to thine eyes, nor slumber to thine eyelids."

Ha! I've got that one down!

Verse 6: "Go to the ant, thou sluggard. Consider her ways, and be wise."

Thanks, I needed that . . .

Good nite all . . . 1:20 A.M., next day, same nite. Amen.

✻ *9:20 P.M., April 20, Weehawken, New Jersey*

**THOUGHT FOR THE DAY:
THERE'S NO SUCH THING AS EX-
WIVES, ONLY ADDITIONAL WIVES.**

✻

We're just across the bridge from New York City, in New Jersey. We had the day off, except I did that interview with Dan Rather. We had a lot of fun telling each other stories. He knows as many as I do.

The Mississippi River is still flooding, and the folks up in Quebec, Canada, at the Summit of the Americas, are protesting in the streets. People from all over the world opposing things—the Free Trade Agreement is one thing that they're against—because they say it's taking jobs away from the working man and only benefits the big corporations. They are also protesting genetically altered foods. It seems like no matter where they try to have their global meeting, people are going to find out about it and show up in great numbers to show their opposition, and stop the meeting if they can.

There has been a lot of tear gas thrown by the police, and people are throwing the same tear gas canisters back at the police, who have so far kept their cool for the most part. There are still a few days left so I hope everything remains relatively calm.

There were these two guys, one a priest and the other just a good ol' boy, who happened to be sitting together on a plane that flew into bad weather. The plane was for sure going to crash. The good ol' boy began to pray saying, "Lord, if you let me live, I'll give half of every-

The Poodiecratic Texas Flag

thing that I've got to the church." The priest overheard his prayer. The plane bounced around and then, miraculously, the sky began to open up and the plane landed safely. The two men got off the plane and the good ol' boy started to walk away. The priest said, "Hey, I thought you promised God if he let you live you'd give half of everything you have to the church. You can just make your check out to me."

The good ol' boy said, "Oh, I made God a better deal. I told him if I ever get back on one of those damned airplanes I'd give him everything."

✯ *11:55 P.M., still the same day*

POODIE AND BUDROCK (or Chicken Dick and Pecker Head, as they lovingly call each other) well, Chicken Dick will be laughing a lot for awhile. Last night on stage when the American flag dropped, Pecker Head had flag duty. At the opening of "Whiskey River" the Texas flag is supposed to drop and the American flag is supposed to drop after the third "one more time" in the second chorus of "Whiskey River." Last night something happened, some sort of malfunction, and when I looked back to see the American flag drop, I saw just a little piece of the American flag flopped down across the star in the Texas flag. Everyone had a good laugh, but I'm sure Chicken Dick will laugh longer than Pecker Head. We are planning on using the photo of the two flags tangled and have it made into a T-shirt. The "Poodiecratic Texas Flag." As you can see, it doesn't take much to entertain us out here.

COACH DARRELL ROYAL is one of the best friends I have, and he's one of the biggest country music fans I know. He introduced me to Mickey

Raphael. I still owe him for that one! Just kidding, Mickey. Just kidding, Coach. More than once he has proven how good a friend he really is. I won't embarrass him by saying too much, but he did invest in the *Red Headed Stranger* movie, along with Ernest Owen, Bill McDavid, and Don Tyson. Coach and Jim Bob Moffat bought my golf course at the IRS auction, but the IRS wouldn't let them keep it. They took it back and sold it to somebody else. But the Coach is a friend, not only to me but to everyone. He'll help anybody.

✳ *12:35 A.M., April 22, next day, same night*

SOMEBODY MY AGE SHOULD BE IN BED. 'Nite all.
Coach Royal's favorite song of mine . . .

Healing Hands of Time

They're working while I'm missing you
Those healing hands of time
And soon they'll be dismissing you
From this heart of mine
They'll lead me safely through the night
And I'll follow as though blind
My future tightly clutched within
Those healing hands of time

They let me close my eyes just then
Those healing hands of time

And soon they'll let me sleep again
Those healing hands of time
So already I've reached mountain peaks
And I've just begun to climb
I'll get over you by clinging to
Those healing hands of time

✳ *May 2, 5:40 P.M.*

I'VE BEEN SICK FOR SEVERAL DAYS, that's the reason I haven't been writing. I've had some kind of bug that's been going around. Everyone on the buses have had it. It's just jumping from one bus to another. As soon as you get better, here it comes again. I tried all of the herbal remedies—pao alto, echinacea, Golden Seal, vitamin C—but it just kept hanging on. I finally got some antibiotics and I'm feeling better. It seems like weeks I've been in a daze, spaced out, and only getting out of my bed to play the show. I haven't missed a date yet, but a lot of them seem vague and hazy.

I hope antibiotics are alright. They say they are OK, but they would say that. I know I haven't been as good as I could be. I'm just glad that I didn't miss any shows. Hopefully I won't, the antibiotics seem to be working.

New York was fantastic. The crowd was a good one. The Beacon Theater is a wonderful place to play, and I think we played OK. I was just beginning to catch whatever I caught. I wasn't 100 percent, but the review of the show in *The New York Times* was exceptionally good. Thank God we made it through New York, New Jersey, Maryland, and Connecticut. It's no fun to be sick anywhere, but out here on the road it's a little different. I can really sympathize with anyone who gets sick out here. At one time or another all of us were down, fortunately not all at once. I hope it's over for us—maybe we can finish the tour.

Bee Spears had to go home to get some tests done. I hope he's doing good. We haven't heard from him since he left, but I'm sure he'll be fine and he'll be back soon. Billy English is playing bass until Bee returns. Billy English can play anything. We're lucky to have him with us.

THERE WAS A GUY who had been in a coma for a long time. They had given up on him ever recovering. He was lying in bed when an aroma came down the hall and into the bedroom. Once the aroma reached his nostrils, he suddenly opened his eyes. It was the smell of his favorite food, chocolate chip cookies. The man awoke and crawled down the hall toward the aroma. Sure enough, when he reached the kitchen, there they were, hot chocolate chip cookies! A favorite that his wife always made him, right on the table cooling. He pulled himself up onto the table to grab one of the cookies. Suddenly, his wife came over, slapped his hand and said, "No, no, honey. These are for the funeral."

Kneel at the Feet of Jesus

Guess I've been hanging around too long
It's just about time I was moving along
I'm gonna kneel at the feet of Jesus
  In the morning
And don't you worry and don't you moan
It's just about time I was moving along

I'm gonna kneel at the feet of Jesus
   In the morning

I'm gonna kneel at the feet of Jesus
   In the morning
Gonna leave this sinful world
Before the dawning
And don't you worry and don't you moan
It's just about time I was moving on
I'm gonna kneel at the feet of Jesus
   In the morning

And when I'm dead and you carry me away
Don't you bury me deep 'cause I ain't gonna stay
I'm gonna kneel at the feet of Jesus
   In the morning
A little bit of dirt and a little bit of gravel
Don't you weigh me down
      'Cause you know I gotta travel
I'm gonna kneel at the feet of Jesus
   In the morning

Going Home

The closer I get to my home, Lord
The more I want to be there
There'll be a gathering of loved ones and friends
And you know I want to be there

There'll be a mixture of teardrops and flowers
        Crying and talking for hours
            About how wild that I was
And if I'd listened to them, I wouldn't be there

Well there's old Charlie Toll
They threw away the mold when they made him
And Jimmy McCline, looks like the wine's
            Finally laid him
And Billy McGray, I could beat any day
            In a card game
And Bessy McNeil, but her tears are real
            I can see pain
There's a mixture of teardrops and flowers
        Crying and talking for hours
            About how wild that I was
And if I'd listened to them, I wouldn't be there

Lord, thanks for the ride
I got a feeling inside that I know you
And if you see your way, you're welcome to stay
'Cause I'm gonna need you
There's a mixture of teardrops and flowers
        Crying and talking for hours
            About how wild that I was
And if I'd listened to them, I wouldn't be there

Here we are in Richmond, Virginia. We've been here three days with the last two days off, and I've had a little time to get better. We play the Landmark Theater tonight. Just finished a sound check and it went pretty good, considering I'm still a bit shaky. The sound in the theater is beautiful. I'm looking forward to the show.

Outside my bus window to the left I see what seems to be a courthouse. All the windows have bars on them. It might be a jail, or maybe just a rough part of town. Maybe it's a cathedral or a church of some kind. I'll probably never know. I'm sure when we leave tonight it'll be dark and late, and I'll never see the front of the building. So, I guess I'll never know unless I ask someone, and that would be cheating.

✳ 1:15 A.M., May 3, on the way to Biloxi

RICHMOND WAS INTO IT TONIGHT. The crowd was so wonderful. I felt better tonight than I have in several days. Thank you, Jesus. We cheated death one more time. I hope Bee Man is OK.

One day Bee told me about when he was a little boy, and his brother went to his mother crying, "Mama, Bee wrote s-h-i-t on my little red wagon."

His mother said, "It's alright. We can wipe it off."

Bee's brother said, "But Mama, he used a fucking nail!"

Bee can tell a joke better than anybody I know. He really gets into it.

BILOXI, MISSISSIPPI, is one of my favorite places. I was in the air force there in 1950. I fell in love with Mississippi—Gulfport, Biloxi—and the whole coastal area.

I first saw Dave Gardner in a place called Gustevens in Gulfport. Back in those days, Biloxi and Gulfport were big gambling towns. They still are, maybe more, now that all the casinos are legal.

Air force days

I was stationed at Kessler AFB for a while. I played at the Airmen's Club, a club for the enlisted personnel at Kessler. I had a lot of fun playing around Biloxi, but I didn't really like the military life. It didn't take long for me to realize that I wasn't cut out for it. But, I still love Biloxi.

Protest Song

I WROTE "JIMMY'S ROAD" when my friend and bass player, David Zettner, was drafted into the army during the Vietnam War. I could have called it "David's Road," but "Jimmy's Road" sounded more euphonious. Thank you, Chet Atkins, for that big word. He said that one time about some line I had written. At the time I didn't know what it meant—words that go together—but I said, "Alright Chet, thanks." I was relieved to find out later it was a good thing.

Jimmy's Road

This is Jimmy's road
Where Jimmy liked to play
And this is Jimmy's grass
Where Jimmy liked to lay around

This is Jimmy's tree
That Jimmy liked to climb
Then Jimmy went to war
And something changed his mind around

This is the battleground
Where Jimmy learned to kill
Now Jimmy has a trade
And Jimmy knows it well—too well
This is Jimmy's grave
Where Jimmy's body lies
And when a soldier falls
Jimmy's body dies—and dies

But this was Jimmy's road
Where Jimmy liked to play
And this is Jimmy's grass
Where Jimmy liked to lay around

I think tonight we're playing at the Grand Casino, and it will finally be warm. I'm sick of all the cold and rain. I've had a couple of relapses trying to play golf in that kind of weather. This will give you an idea of how smart I am: If I had to work outside in that mess I would bitch and moan, but there's something about golf that makes idiots of us all I suppose.

Rainy Day Blues

Well it's cloudy in the morning
Gonna be raining in the afternoon
I said it's cloudy in the morning
Gonna be raining in the afternoon
And if you don't like this rainy weather
You better pack your bags and move

But if you're running from it, brother
The only road that I can see
If you're running from it, brother
The only road that I can see
Is the road that leads to nowhere
And nowhere is a fool like me

Rain keep a-falling
Falling on my window pane
Rain keep a-falling
Falling on my window pane
Never seen so much rainy weather
Guess I'll never see the sun again

Better save those dimes and nickels
Save 'em for a rainy day
You'd better save your dimes and nickels
Save 'em for a rainy day
It ain't gonna keep the rain from coming
But at least you know you've paid your way

THESE GUYS WERE playing golf one day when a funeral passed by on the road next to the golf course. One of the players took off his hat and waited until the funeral procession passed. One of his fellow golfers said, "John, that's mighty respectable of you to do that."

The guy said, "It's the least I can do for her. We would have been married twenty years today."

✳ *11:45 P.M., May 3*

THIS WAS A DAY OFF IN BILOXI. It turned into a long drive from Richmond. I spent the day, well what's left of it (we didn't get here until four), swimming a little, running a little, and practicing my tae kwan do. David Anderson and I walked next door to the Waffle House before watching the last of the Mavericks basketball game. What a game! The Mavericks pulled it out after being down seventeen points at halftime. I was happy for Don Nelson and the Mavericks. Don and I are very good friends. He has a house in Maui and we have some fun poker games at my place on Monday nights. He's a wonderful person and I'm proud to call him my friend.

David Anderson is my long-time trusted friend and employee, whose talents are many and who does so many different things well, from computers to settling up with the promoter. His birthday is just before mine, so he always manages to get overlooked. He wants it that way, but happy birthday, David. I don't know how old he is but he was a child when he came to work for us, and he's no child today. None of us are. The road has a way of aging you a little faster.

David and I cowrote a song together.

My Broken Heart Belongs to You

I lost my mind so long ago
I wanted everyone to know
I wanted everyone to see
My broken heart belongs to me

I'd go beyond the thought of you
And a broken heart was nothing new
I wanted everyone to see
My broken heart belonged to me

And now that autumn fills the air
I feel your presence everywhere
Now my fears are coming true
My broken heart belongs to you

Talked to Ray Price today. We're going into the studio this Monday to do another album. I'm sure looking forward to that. He's still the best singer in country music. He wants to do an album of songs written by Texas writers and call it "The Texas Album." We'll certainly have a lot of writers to choose from: Floyd Tillman, Leon Payne, Lefty Frizzell, Bob Wills, and many, many more. We'll record it at World Headquarters in Luck, the same place we recorded *Rainbow Connection*. It's a small, all-digital studio, and the sound is fantastic.

❋ *12:29 A.M., May 4, same night, next day (I know, it's complicated. Just don't think about it.)*

GOOD NIGHT.

❋ *Sunday, May 7, 12:25 A.M.*

JUST FINISHED PLAYING MEMPHIS. We played a huge festival right downtown. Bob Dylan was playing a mile down the street on another stage, right after the Black Crowes. What a hot crowd!

I also went into the studio this afternoon with T. G. Sheppard and recorded a song called "It's Texas." I liked the song, and T. G. and his folks were very nice. I also did a radio interview with a station here in Memphis. They had an advance copy of *Rainbow Connection* and say they like it.

On our way to Austin for a couple of days off before we go into the studio again with Ray Price . . .

DID YOU HEAR the one about Billy Roy the cabin boy?

> *The dirty little ripper*
> *He lined his ass with broken glass*
> *And circumcised the skipper*

Or,

> *My name is Joe Bailey*
> *My dick is a whalie*
> *and my balls weigh ninety-four pounds*
> *If you know a lady*
> *who wants a nice baby*
> *just tell her Joe Bailey's in town*

I'M SORRY, but if I go ahead and get them all out, maybe I won't think of them again. I've got to remember to call preacher Gerald Mann tomorrow. He always has a couple of good jokes for me. Joke-telling is therapeutic in a sick kind of way. Laughter is still the best medicine.

If you ain't crazy, there's something wrong with you.

———

We just passed Little Rock, Arkansas, and that should put us in Austin about noon tomorrow or today, depending on how you look at your watch. It's already tomorrow, but it's still tonight.

No Tomorrow in Sight

The children are sleeping
Our talk can begin
We've waited until they've gone to bed
We knew they would cry
When we said goodbye
And I'd rather leave quietly instead

We can never be happy
We both know it's true
We've quarrelled from the day that we met
Our love was too weak
To pull our dreams through
But too strong to let us forget

I hope we can salvage a few memories
To carry us through the long nights
The clock's striking midnight
Yesterday's gone and there's no tomorrow in sight

In our efforts to break through
The thick walls of pride

With harsh words that burned to the core
The walls still remain
But the words broke inside
And strengthened the walls even more

I hope we can salvage a few memories
To carry us through the long nights
The clock's striking midnight
Yesterday's gone and there's no tomorrow in sight

I wrote that way back in the early '60s. Very few people have even heard it because sad songs and waltzes weren't selling that year.

Sad Songs and Waltzes

I'm writing a song all about you
A true song as real as my tears
    But you've no need to fear it
    For no one will hear it
Cause sad songs and waltzes aren't selling this year

I'll tell all about how you cheated
I'd like for the whole world to hear
    I'd like to get even
    With you cause you're leaving
But sad songs and waltzes aren't selling this year

It's a good thing that I'm not a star
You don't know how lucky you are
 Though my record may say it
 No one will play it
Cause sad songs and waltzes aren't selling this year

Both of these songs put together probably sold about four copies. That's not the important thing. To me, just getting the words out of my head and onto paper was an exercise worth performing. Those kinds of thoughts left bottled up inside can do more damage than good, and can probably cause everything from cancer to heart break. Sometimes just saying the words can cause some kind of healing to begin. But if you sing those songs every night year after year, I believe you can also prevent a total healing because you're always opening old wounds.

So what's the answer? Who knows. If you have a hit with a sad song, just remember when you wrote it, it was for you. When you sing it over and over and over, it's for the benefit of the listener. Don't let it spoil an otherwise good night. Attempt to sing the song for the audience, and try not to get too involved in it yourself. It's a very thin line, and a lot easier said than done.

Sometimes I believe the reason a lot of country singers and writers have gone off the deep end was because they could not find that thin line, and could never fully recover from the evening that caused them to write the song in the beginning. Hank Williams, Floyd Tillman, George Jones, Lefty Frizzell, and myself included, could in some way be victims of our own words.

Man with the Blues

If you need some advice in being lonely
If you need a little help in feeling blue
If you need some advice on how to cry all night
Come to me, I'm the man with the blues

I'm the man with a hundred thousand heartaches
And I've got most every color of the blues
So if you need a little shove in foulin' up in love
Come to me, I'm the man with the blues

I'm the man with a hundred thousand teardrops
And I've got a good selection old and new

If you need some advice in being lonely
If you need a little help in feeling blue
If you need some advice on how to cry all night
Come to me, I'm the man with the blues

You Ought to Hear Me Cry

If you think I laugh louder than anyone here
If you think that my volume's too high
If you think I laugh loud
You ain't heard nothing yet
You ought to hear me cry

I go home to a home where love's almost gone
Not enough to fill one needle's eye
> *Then I sit down in a corner*
> *And I turn on the tears*
And you ought to hear me cry

If you think I talk louder than maybe I should
Well, I guess I'm that kind of guy
> *But if I talk loud and laugh loud*
> *You ain't heard it all*
You ought to hear me cry

Slow Down Old World

Slow down, slow down
Old world, there's no hurry
'Cause my life ain't mine anymore
I lived too fast
Now it's too late to worry
> *And I'm too blue to cry anymore*

I once was a fool for the women
Now I'm just a fool, nothing more
So slow down, slow down
> *Old world, there's no hurry*
'Cause my life ain't mine anymore

I once had a way with the women
Till one got away with my heart

So slow down, slow down
   Old world there's no hurry
'Cause my life ain't mine anymore

And here's a little toe-tapper . . .

I Just Can't Let You Say Goodbye

I had not planned on seeing you
I was afraid of what I'd do
But pride is strong, here am I
And I just can't let you say goodbye

Please have no fear, you're in no harm
As long as you're here in my arms
But you can't leave so please don't try
But I just can't let you say goodbye

What force behind your evil mind
Can let your lips speak so unkind
To one who loves as much as I
But I just can't let you say goodbye

The flesh around your throat is pale
Indented by my fingernails
Please don't scream and please don't cry
'Cause I just can't let you say goodbye

Your voice is still, it speaks no more
You'll never hurt me anymore
Death is a friend to love and I
'Cause now you'll never say goodbye

BEE MAN WAS BACK TONIGHT! The doctors say all the tests were negative, and in medical testing, negative is good. It seems like it should be the other way around. Negative is bad. Positive is good. Oh well, I hope they know what the hell they're doing. I wonder if a doctor would ever tell his patient to think positive? Hell, in medical terms, that could maybe kill you. I never could understand why an airport is called a terminal. Terminal sounds bad to me. Terminal sounds negative as hell. It's way too deep a subject for such a shallow mind, so let's move on.

THE DOCTORS CAME in and told the patient, "Got some good news, and some bad news. Which do you want first?"

The guy said, "Tell me the bad news first."

The doc said, "You have an incurable disease and you'll probably be dead in three weeks."

The guy said, "What in the hell is the good news?"

The doctor said, "Did you see that good-looking blond nurse when you came into the office?"

The guy said yes.

The doctor said, "Well I'm fucking her."

✳ *2:10 A.M., same night, next day*

I'M GOING TO BED TO TRY AND SLEEP this off. Maybe I'll wake up with a clean mind, or maybe I won't. I'll be happy just to wake up. Remember, halitosis is better than no breath at all. Thank you, Lord, for making me your guinea pig. I guess you wanted to see how sick and perverted one son of a bitch can be. I'll try not to disappoint you. 'Nite all . . .

P.S. THE BAD part about smoking weed . . .

1. It's too expensive. It costs more than gold.
2. Over usage will cause you to get bronchitis.
3. You'll smell like a skunk.
4. Everytime someone says anything negative about smoking pot, you become somewhat hostile and start yakking about how hemp could save the world, and you start quoting page after page of *The Emperor Wears No Clothes,* and you wind up only sounding like a pothead trying to justify your habit.

My advice would be to just cut back and shut up. Amen.

AND OH, yeah—

5. It's still illegal.

So when someone tells you there's nothing wrong with smoking pot, tell them to kiss your ass 'cause you know better. But it's still the best natural medicine in the world. So use it, don't abuse it.

GOD HAS BLESSED you richly, so get down on your knees and thank Him. Don't forget the less fortunate or God will personally kick your ass. I'd love to do it for Him, but I can't be everywhere.

Amen.

TWO THINGS I can't stand. One is somebody standing there with a cigarette hanging out of their mouth and a glass of whiskey in one hand, saying how bad smoking pot is for you, and the other is a fat doctor telling you not to run because it can be hard on your knees. These are some of the guys who are in for a divine butt-kicking.

And as my first wife, Martha, used to say, "Don't worry about a thing 'cause there ain't nothing going to be alright." Hence the title of my book, *The Facts of Life and Other Dirty Jokes,* and don't forget the words from the gospel according to Hank Williams, "I'll never get out of this world alive."

✳ *3:05 A.M*

OK. 1-2-3, everybody sleep.

POODIE SAYS IT'S ALRIGHT TO STEP ON YOUR DICK, JUST DON'T STAND ON IT.

✳ *1:45 A.M., May 12*

JUST FINISHED A FUN GIG in Marksville, Louisiana, maybe one of our best. I also just finished the Ray Price album. It came out so good! I can tell you Ray is singing so fine you won't believe it. Only five weeks ago at Red's hospital, Hermann Hospital, in Houston, he was split down the middle for an aneurism. A few miracles later he is singing his ass off at World Headquarters in Luck, with Dr. Red Duke standing there listening to every note. I said it before and I'll say it again: Ray Price is the greatest country singer ever, period.

We recorded "I've Just Destroyed the World I'm Living In," a song he and I wrote years ago, and "Soft Rain," a song written by Ray. I could have had half the song.

I was on the road, working for Ray. He was up front working on a song and I was in the back of the bus playing poker with Jimmy Day, Pete Wade, and Shorty Lavender. Ray said, "Come on up here, hoss, and help me finish this song."

I said, "Hell, I can make more money right here playing poker."

I missed helping Ray write "Soft Rain" and lost two hundred dollars playing poker. The song went on to become a huge #1 hit for Ray.

Back then, Ray was raising fighting roosters and racehorses. I heard he had horses that fought and roosters that ran, however, I never believed that.

Back to my story . . .

Ray called me one day and asked if he could bring out one of his fighting roosters and leave him to exercise. I said, "Fine, but my wife, Shirley, has some good laying hens. Will he hurt them?"

Ray said, "Oh no, it won't bother those hens at all." The next day, Shirley went out to feed her hens and one lay dead in the chicken pen. I called Ray, told him what happened, and he said, "OK, I'll come get the rooster." He didn't.

The next day, same thing, another dead hen. Shirley was so mad she came out of the house with my shotgun. I knew she would have probably accidentally killed everything on the farm except the rooster, especially with that gun. I took the gun and shot the rooster. I called Ray, who was pretty mad. He said, "That fighting cock was worth a hell of a lot of money."

I said, "Raymond, [he hates it when I call him Raymond] there ain't a fighting rooster alive that's worth one good laying hen."

He wouldn't speak to me for a long time. We've both gotten a lot of mileage out of the story. It's fallen into the "no good deed goes unpunished" category.

I'VE GOT TO WRITE this down before I forget it. Mark Rothbaum, my manager, was just reminding me of a David Allan Coe story. David Allan was being booked by the Shorty Lavender Talent Agency in Nashville. One night, David Allan mooned the audience. The local promoter called Shorty, who called Mark (who was also managing David Allan). Shorty was hot! He said, "Nobody drops their pants on a Shorty Lavender date!"

Back to the album . . .

We did Floyd Tillman's "I'll Keep on Loving You," which he wrote about his car, and "This Cold War with You," one of the best songs ever written. Also we recorded the Fred Rose songs "Home in San Antone," "Deep Water," and "It Wouldn't Be the Same Without You." Fred Rose also wrote "Blue Eyes Crying in the Rain." We did a Fred Foster song called "Run That By Me One More Time," a bluegrass tune. We did my song, "I'm Still Not Over You," "I'm So Ashamed," and "Something to Think About." Come to think of it, I scored pretty good on this. Five out of ten, it could have been six. Should have been six if I had not blown it with "Soft Rain." I'm very happy with the way the CD has turned out.

It Wouldn't Be the Same Without You

I could wander the byways that we wandered
     through
But it wouldn't be the same without you
These familiar old places would just make me blue
But it wouldn't be the same without you

I wasted my love on a careless romance
But I'd do it again if I had the chance
I could start my life over with somebody new
But it wouldn't be the same without you

I've Just Destroyed the World I'm Living In

The sun just went behind the clouds
There's darkness all around me now
I've just destroyed the world I'm living in

I broke her heart so many times
And now at last I've broken mine
I've just destroyed the world I'm living in

What made me think that I could go on hurting
*   her*
I should have known there had to be an end
Fools in love are taught by fate
We never learn till it's too late
I've just destroyed the world I'm living in

I'm So Ashamed

I'm so ashamed of my eyes 'cause they still cry
*   for you*
After they both watched my hand wave good-bye
*   to you*
I've told them time and time again this will
*   never do*
I've told them how you always laugh at teardrops

I'm so ashamed
Of my arms for missing you
Last night I woke up just in time to feel them reach
*   for you*
And now my heart confesses it still wants you too
I'm so ashamed of them all for loving you

Something to Think About

You're wondering just what I'll do
Now that it's over and done
Well that's something to think about
And I've already begun

I suppose that I'll find a way
People usually do
But it's something to think about
I'll be lost without you

One thing I would have you do
Please consider the dawn
The dawn of your lonely years
When youth and beauty are gone

And when you can no longer have
Any sweetheart you choose
Here's something to think about
I'll still be thinking of you

I'm Still Not Over You

Today I made a point to go somewhere I knew
*   you'd be*
I had to know if you still had the same effect on me

And the moment that I saw you there I knew
No matter what I do
I'm still not over you
I'm still not over you, that feeling's still the same
I'm still not over you, I find that nothing's changed
And perhaps someday I'll find somebody new
But no matter what I do
I'm still not over you

✳ 2:20 A.M.

I'M SUPPOSED TO TEE OFF today at 8 A.M. back in Austin for a bene-fit golf game. I'll have fun. Coach Darrell Royal, Bobby Day, and more good friends will be there playing for our Montessori school. They'll be there to support the school, plus we all love to play golf.

Paul and I played Bee and David yesterday afternoon in Louisiana. There were seventy-two sand traps. We hit them all. It was a good course though, and right next to the casino, making it handy too.

✳ May 13, Mothers Day, on our way to Waco

A LADY WENT INTO A DRUGSTORE asking if they had Viagra. The pharmacist said yes, and she asked, "Have you ever tried it?"

He said he had. She then asked, "Can you get it over the counter?"

He said, "I think I could . . . if I took two."

———

A FAN TOLD ME he took one every night just to keep from falling out of bed.

They say Viagra can make a lawyer taller. Hell, this could go on forever.

I'M SITTING HERE on the bus listening to the stuff by me and Ray Price. It's still sounding pretty good. Tonight is a benefit for the hospital in Whitney, Texas. My friend Donald Reed had asked that we do one, and I was glad to be able to help out, especially a good buddy like Donald. We went to school together in Abbott and graduated together. He was the valedictorian and I was just glad to be there. So tonight I look forward to seeing him and all my old schoolmates from Abbott High.

I talked to Jackie Clements, he's planning on being at the show tonight. Jackie's also an old school buddy. We've all spent the night at each other's houses many times in our school years. Old friends are the best friends, and there ain't many any older than we are.

I don't mean to start anything this late in the game, but I still think his wife, Fayedell, would have chosen me over Jackie if Jackie hadn't had a car and had her so brainwashed. Oh well, all's fair in love and war. She probably did the right thing. Traveling around with me for forty years would have been a lot of fun I'm sure, but I'm afraid the diesel fumes from the bus would have eventually proven too much for such a sweet and sensitive person.

It looks like we're getting to the end of the book, so I'll start winding down. I picked up a book one time and started reading it. The first paragraph said that everything we do, we've done a million times before. So I put the book down. No need in doing that again. I personally

saved that bit of information until the last paragraph of this book. I
didn't want to lose you.

✸ *6:15 P.M.*

I KNOW IT'S TOO early to go to bed, but this is Waco. Good night, all.

> *Jesus was a Baylor Bear*
> *But Jesus wouldn't cut his hair*
> *His helmet didn't fit, but he didn't give a shit*
> *'Cause Jesus was a Baylor Bear*
> *Amen*

Pick Up the Tempo

> *People are saying that time will take care*
> *Of people like me*
> *And that I'm living too fast and they say I can't last*
> *For much longer*
> *But little they see that their thoughts of me*
> *Is my savior*
> *And little they know that the beat ought to go*
> *Just a little faster*
>
> *So pick up the tempo just a little*
> *And take it on home*

The singer ain't singing
And the drummer's been dragging
    Too long
Time will take of itself so just leave time alone
And pick up the tempo just a little
    And take it on home

Well I'm wild and mean, I'm creating a scene
    I'm goin' crazy
Well I'm good and bad and I'm happy and sad
    And I'm lazy
I'm quiet and I'm loud and I'm gathering a crowd
    And I like gravy
I'm 'bout half off the wall but I learned it all
    In the Navy

So pick up the tempo just a little
    And take it on home
The singer ain't singing
And the drummer's been dragging
    Too long
Time will take of itself so just leave time alone
And pick up the tempo just a little
    And take it on home

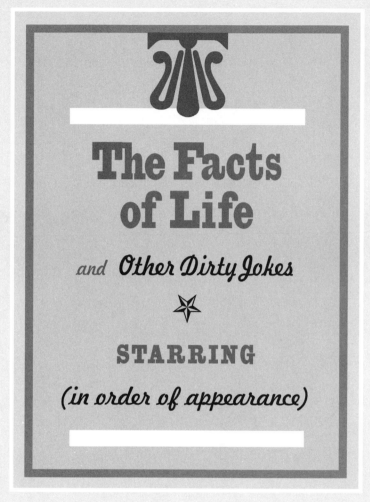

The Facts of Life

and **Other Dirty Jokes**

✦

STARRING

(in order of appearance)

Roger Miller

Bob Wills

Lana and Willie

Kinky Friedman

Honeysuckle Rose III

Ben Dorcy

Waylon Payne

Jody Payne

Sammi Smith

Mama Nelson

Daddy Nelson

Ira Nelson

Myrle Nelson Harvey

Lorraine and Willie

Mother Earth

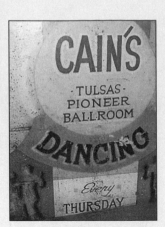

Cain's Ballroom

Jackie King

Zeke Varner

Bud Fletcher and the Texans

Steve, Willie, and Albert

Sheriff Jack Harwell

Hank Williams

Paul Buskirk

Claude Gray

DJ Bill Mack and guest Pete Stamper

Billy Walker

Jesus

Joey Floyd and Willie

Casey Tibbs

John Wayne, Ben Dorcy, Maureen O'Hara

Minnie Pearl,
Ann-Margret

Buck Owens

Hank Thompson

**Billy Deaton, Ray Price,
Shorty Lavender**

Pat Green

Dr. Red Duke

Dr. Booger Nelson

Trigger

Bobbie and Willie

Lee Ann Womack

Matt Serletic, Willie, and Brian McKnight

Willie and Mark Rothbaum

The Jordanaires, 1961

Harlan Howard, Buck White

Frances Preston and Willie

Mel Tillis

Charlie Dick, DJ Mike Hoyer

Patsy Cline

Little Jimmy Dickens

Willie, 1961

Signing to the Grand Ole Opry, with Haze Jones and Ott Devine

Hank Snow

Chubby Wise

Billy Deaton and Faron Young

Hank Cochran

Sister Bobbie and her sons Randy and Michael

Paula Carleen, Connie, and Willie

Jerry Jeff Walker

Steve Fromholz

Gary P. Nunn

Waylon Jennings

Hazel Smith

Billy Joe Shaver

Willie, Bee, Paul, and Poodie

Scooterville, USA

Dandalion and Daffy

Randy Travis

Ralph Emery

Willie and Kris Kristofferson

George Strait

Ernest Tubb, Tommy Collins, Merle Haggard

Johnny Cash

The Geezinslaw Brothers

Bob Cole, Sammy Allred

Scott, the editor

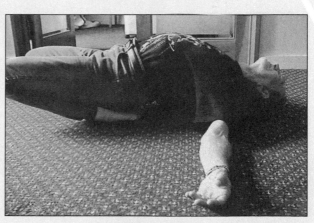

Willie relaxing

Jim Henson

Katie, Willie, and Jill

Willie, 1955

Gene Autry

Roy Rogers

The Durango Kid

Elvis Presley, Hank Snow

Johnny Gimble

Willie and Django

Paul Corbin

Bill Wittliff

Smiley Burnette

The Red Headed Stranger

Willie and Morgan
Fairchild

Katharine Ross, Bryan Fowler,
and Julian Shay, aka Willie

Carolyn Mugar,
Rachel Fowler

Martha Fowler, Matt
Hubbard, and Dean

Hog Farming Willie, 1968

Dan Rather

Willie and John T. Flores

Willie, 1983

Chicken Dick

Pecker Head

Darrell and Edith Royal

Bee Spears

BONGO NAKED OR UNTIL THE COPS COME

Mickey Raphael

David Zettner

Floyd Tillman

Lefty Frizzell

Willie and Ray Price

Tony Lyons, T. G. Sheppard

Shirley Nelson

David Allan Coe

Fred Rose

Jackie Clements

Fayedell Clements

The Band

Bee Spears, bass

Bobbie Nelson, piano

Jackie King, guitar

Mickey Raphael, harmonica

Paul English, drums

**Jody Payne,
guitar and vocals**

Bill English, percussion

The Crew

Poodie Locke, Prettiest Baby in Waco, 1952

David Anderson, aka Fallopian Muldoon

Larry Gorham, security: "Tread on This."

Tunin' Tom Hawkins

Kenny Koepke, reason for "the Kenny Clause"

Scooter Franks, mayor of Scooterville

James Franks, Scooterville city manager

Gates Moore, Honeysuckle Rose III driver: "Tough, but oh so gentle."

**Tony Sizemore, crew bus,
aka Man of Steel**

**Rick "Mike" Moher,
equipment truck:
"You build it, I'll park it."**

**Neil Smidt, band bus,
aka The New Guy**

Sound, Lights, Camera . . .

**Bobby Lemons,
sound**

**Dan Laveglia,
sound**

Action!

Buddy Prewitt, lights

Ben Dorcy, action

Family Shots

Great-granddaughter Lauren

Great-granddaughter Andrea Lee

Granddaughters
Rachel and Martha

Daughters Amy and Paula

Rachel, Paula, Willie, and Amy

Anthony and Rebecca with their mom, Susie, at Rebecca's wedding

Raelyn and Grandpa

Grandsons Nelson and Bryan

The End

PHOTO CREDITS

Featured Photographs

Page 59: Photograph provided courtesy of Farm Aid.

Page 85: Photograph provided courtesy of the Country Music Hall of Fame and Museum.

Page 101: Photograph provided courtesy of Ralph Emery Productions.

Page 120, Page 133: Photographs provided courtesy of Lana Nelson.

Page 148: Photograph provided courtesy of Alive Films.

All other featured photographs provided courtesy of the Lana Nelson Collection.

Cast of Characters

The following photographs provided courtesy of Les Leverett: Roger Miller; Billy Walker; DJ Bill Mack; John Wayne, Ben Dorcy, and Maureen O'Sullivan; Minnie Pearl and Ann-Margret; Hank Thompson; Billy Deaton, Ray Price, and Shorty Lavender; The Jordanaires; Harlan Howard and Buck White; Mel Tillis; Charlie Dick and DJ Mike Hoyer; Patsy Cline; Little Jimmy Dickens; Willie, 1961; Signing to the Grand Ole Opry, with Haze Jones and Ott Devine; Hank Snow; Chubby Wise; Billy Deaton and Faron Young; Waylon Jennings; Ernest Tubb, Tommy Collins, and Merle Haggard; Johnny Cash; Jim Henson; Elvis Presley and Hank Snow; Johnny Gimble; Paul Corbin; Tony Lyons and T. G. Sheppard; Shirley Nelson; and David Allan Coe.

The following photographs provided courtesy of the Les Leverett Collection: Willie, 1955; Gene Autry; Roy Rogers; *The Durango Kid;* and Fred Rose.

The following photographs provided courtesy of Lana Nelson: Honeysuckle Rose III; Ben Dorcy; Waylon Payne; Jody Payne; Cain's Ballroom; Jackie King; Steve, Willie, and Albert; Jesus; Joey Floyd; Casey Tibbs; Sister Bobbie and her sons Randy and Michael; Willie, Bee, Paul, and Poodie; Scooterville, USA; Dandalion and Daffy; Willie relaxing; Katie, Willie, and Jill; Willie and Django; Martha Fowler, Matt Hubbard, and Dean; Dan Rather; Chicken Dick; Pecker Head; Mickey Raphael; Bee Spears; David Zettner; Bongo Naked T-shirt; Floyd Tillman; Willie and Ray Price; all photos of "The Band," pages 224–25; Poodie Locke; David Anderson; Larry Gorham; Tunin' Tom Hawkins; Gates Moore; Bobby Lemons; Buddy Prewitt; Ben Dorcy; great-granddaughter Lauren; great-granddaughter Andrea Lee; Granddaughters Rachel and Martha; Willie and Bobbie performing.

The following photographs provided courtesy of the Lana Nelson Collection: Bob Wills; Sammi Smith; Mama Nelson; Daddy Nelson; Bud Fletcher and the Texans; Sheriff Jack Harwell; Hank Williams; Pat Green; Dr. Red Duke; Dr. Booger Nelson; Trigger; Bobbie and Willie; Frances Preston and Willie; Paula Carleen, Connie, and Willie; Billy Joe Shaver; George Strait; Willie, 1955; Smiley Burnette; Bill Wittliff; Carolyn Mugar and Rachel Fowler; Hog Farming Willie, 1968; Willie, 1983; Darrell and Edith Royal; Jackie Clements; Fayedell Clements; and Grandsons Nelson and Bryan.

The following photographs provided courtesy of David Anderson: Lana and Willie; Zeke Varner; Paul Buskirk; Matt Serletic, Willie, and Brian McKnight; Willie and Mark Rothbaum; Willie and John T. Flores; Kenny Koepke; Scooter Franks; James Franks; Tony Sizemore; Neil Smidt; Rick "Mike" Moher; and Dan Laveglia.

The following photographs provided courtesy of Scott Newton:Ira Nelson; Myrle Nelson Harvey; Jerry Jeff Walker (1979); Steve Fromholz (1975); and Gary P. Nunn (1975).

Photograph of Kinky Friedman provided courtesy of Don Imus / Fuji Films.

Photograph of Lorraine Nelson and Willie provided courtesy of George Fowler.

Photograph of Mother Earth provided courtesy of NASA.

Photographs of Claude Gray and Lefty Frizzell provided courtesy of the Country Music Hall of Fame and Museum.

Photograph of Buck Owens provided courtesy of Buck Owens Productions.

Photograph of Lee Ann Womack provided courtesy of Tony Baker.

Photograph of Hank Cochran provided courtesy of Jim Shea.

Photograph of Hazel Smith provided courtesy of Michael Arnaud.

Photograph of Ralph Emery provided courtesy of Ralph Emery Productions.

Photograph of Randy Travis provided courtesy of Michael Tackett.

Photograph of Willie and Kris Kristofferson provided courtesy of CBS / Sony.

Photograph of the Geezinslaw Brothers provided courtesy of James J. Kriegsmann.

Photograph of Bob Cole and Sammy Allred provided courtesy of Ted S. Warren.

Photograph of "Scott, the editor" provided courtesy of Harvey Wang.

The following photographs provided courtesy of Alive Films: The Read Headed Stranger; Willie and Morgan Fairchild; and Katharine Ross, Bryan Fowler, and Julian Shay, aka Willie.

Photograph of "Daughters Amy and Paula" provided courtesy of the Jimmy Carter Library.

Photograph of "Rachel, Paula, Willie, and Amy" provided courtesy of Charles Wilkins.

Photograph of "Anthony and Rebecca with mom, Susie, at Rebecca's wedding" and "Raelyn and Grandpa" provided courtesy of Susie Nelson.